# NOODLES
# EXPRESS

# NOODLES EXPRESS

## *by* DANA McCAULEY

**Fast and Easy Meals in
15 to 45 minutes**

Random House of Canada
*A Denise Schon Book*

For Oliver, whose unconventional table manners and unlikely enthusiasm for bold flavors make him my favorite tiny guy!

## Random House of Canada

Copyright © 1999 Denise Schon Books Inc.
Text copyright © 1999 Dana McCauley
Illustrations copyright © 1999 Huntley/Muir
Front cover photograph copyright © 1999
Hal Roth Photography Inc.

Published in Canada in 1999 by
Random House of Canada Limited, Toronto

Published in the United States of America by Firefly Books

Canadian Cataloguing in Publication Data

McCauley, Dana
  Noodles express

Includes index.
ISBN 0-679-31017-7  (2nd print. with corr.)

1. Cookery (Pasta). 2. Noodles. 3. Quick and easy cookery. I. Title.

TX809.M17M325 1999      641.8'22      C98-930923-1

Cover photo: Stir-Fried Jewels over Chow Mein, p. 57
Design: Counterpunch/Linda Gustafson
Editorial: Shaun Oakey
Index: Barbara Schon

Printed and bound in China
10  9  8  7  6  5  4  3  2  1

A Denise Schon Book

# CONTENTS

List of Recipes    7

Introduction    9

What Is Time?    11

Five Things You Should Know    12

About Noodles    16

## RECIPES

15 MINUTES    18

30 MINUTES    84

45 MINUTES    132

Acknowledgments    156

Index    157

# LIST OF RECIPES

Aromatic Leek, Soba and Shiitake Soup, 90

Asian Pear Salad with Cranberry Dressing, 86

Asian Pesto and Noodles, 74

Asparagus, Tarragon and Lemon Fettuccine, 102

Broad Noodles with Mushroom Port Sauce, 136

Bucatini with Tamari-Almond Sauce, 62

Buttermilk-Walnut Quick Gratin, 78

Campfire Sweet Potato and Pasta Salad, 37

Caramelized Onion, Green Bean and Fusilli Toss, 146

Chili with Pasta and Two Beans, 150

Chow Mein Salad with Citrus Dressing, 32

Coconut Jade Stir-Fry, 98

Creamy Mexican Pasta Dinner, 122

Creamy Wasabi Pasta and Red Bean Salad, 45

Curried Orzo Salad, 42

Dana's Dan Dan Noodles, 63

Easy Cous Cous Salad with Sherry Vinaigrette, 108

Egg Noodles Marengo, 140

Embarrassingly Easy Asian-Style Pasta Primavera, 67

Fast and Fresh Fettuccine, 71

Fettuccine Sultana, 80

Fiery Coconut Noodle Soup, 88

Firecracker Noodles, 116

Five-Minute Tomato Ramen Soup, 23

Fresh Pea and Egg Noodle Soup, 22

Gnocchi with Rich Carrot Cardamom Sauce, 138

Green Curry and Green Apple Salad, 30

Honey-Glazed Snap Peas and Noodles, 66

Hot and Sour Soup and Noodle Supper, 20

Hot Mustard Sauce Chow Mein, 56

Macaroni and Lentil Salad, 44

Malaysian Coconut Salad, 134

Mango and Rice Noodle Salad in Lettuce Cups, 50

Mushroom and Noodle Snack in Lemon Broth, 25

Noodles in Mushroom Ginger Broth, 28

Noodles with Asian Roasted Red Pepper Sauce, 52

Noodles with Fennel and Creamy
    Star Anise–Beet Sauce, 112

One-Pan Gingered Ratatouille and Ditali, 152

Orange-Infused Beet and Orecchiette Salad, 40

Orzo Goreng, 48

Pacific Rim Stove-top Noodle Quiche, 142

Painted Desert Pasta Salad, 34

Pan-Asian Penne all'Arrabbiata, 114

Pangaea Capellini, 128

Pasta Shells with Bombay Sauce, 154

Pasta with Spring Onion Sauce, 126

Peas and Potatoes with Orecchiette, 70

Penne, Asparagus and Yellow Peppers with
    Champagne-Saffron Vinaigrette, 38

Penne with Middle Eastern Eggplant Sauce, 144

Plaid Noodles, 118

Pomegranate Cous Cous in Pitas, 46

Quick Skillet Macaroni and Cheese, 64

Red Curry–Coconut Stir-Fry, 58

Red Curry Broth with Oodles of Noodles, 31

Ruby-Stained Fusilli with Lemon and Dill, 92

Sesame Noodles, 54

Shanghai Noodles in Orange Sauce, 124

Skoo-Bi-Do Rapini with Pine Nuts and Currants, 104

Snow Pea and Mushroom Stir-Fry
   in Black Bean Sauce, 68

Soba Salad with Tamari Dressing and Broccoli, 36

Spaghetti with Minted Pea Sauce, 83

Spice Tent Orzo, 76

Spicy Spaghetti and Vegetable Toss, 96

Spinach Noodles with Spicy Green Curry, 82

Spinach with Capellini in Chili-Ginger Sauce, 72

Spoon and Fork Asian Noodle Soup, 26

Squash Ravioli Meunière
   with Pine Nuts and Capers, 77

Stir-Fried Broccoli and Tofu with Rice Ribbons, 110

Stir-Fried Jewels over Chow Mein, 57

Superlative Vegetable Chow Mein, 60

Super Szechwan Tofu and Noodle Supper, 100

Sweet and Sour Peppers and Farfalle Stir-Fry, 120

Tagliatelle with Wasabi Cream Sauce, 51

Thai Marinated Eggplant and Mushrooms
   with Rice Noodles, 148

Toronto Meets Singapore Noodles, 94

Tortellini Salad à la Grecque, 39

20-Minute Vegetarian Pad Thai, 130

Vietnamese Rice Sticks with Vegetables
   and Peanut Sauce, 106

Zesty Pasta Salad with Peppery Greens, 35

Zippy Ramen, 24

# INTRODUCTION

While I was expecting my son, Oliver, I spent a lot of my time thinking about what to eat next. At the time my husband, Martin, and I lived in the heart of downtown Toronto, where every imaginable type of restaurant was a mere stone's throw from our balcony. Within a mile I could find Indian, Ethiopian, Vietnamese, Japanese, Filipino, Greek, Chinese, Middle Eastern or any other ethnic restaurant. Besides the expected franchises, many of these eateries were owned and operated by people whose menus focused on the food of their homeland. That meant that if I ordered adventurously and asked a few probing questions each meal could be educational, too. I'll confess that I gained more than 40 pounds during my pregnancy. By the time I entered my second trimester I was a devoted regular at many of these great neighborhood restaurants.

But it was the noodle houses of downtown Toronto that really stole my heart. These fine establishments offered delicious, nutritious Asian noodle concoctions in stir-fries or in broth for very low prices – which meant that even a person with a hearty appetite like mine could afford to eat out several times a week. In fact, if I'd stuck to eating only noodles and hadn't been compelled to stop in at Papaya Hut each day for a large Strawberry-Piña Colada smoothie, I'd have had a lot less aprés-baby weight to lose!

My love affair with noodles continued well into the post-partum period. Unfortunately, my new sidekick and the cold winter weather curtailed my usual pilgrimages to the neighborhood noodle shops. Having no alternative, I started to cook noodles for myself, and most of the time the result was a meatless meal since I often didn't make the time to shop for fresh meat or fish.

I'm not a vegetarian in the traditional sense; on the contrary, I can be a raving carnivore on the right day. But like so many others, I don't like to eat meat on a daily basis anymore. So, if you're a vegan or a strict vegetarian who will not eat a dish that contains dairy or a small amount of fish sauce, close this book and give it to a friend. My recipes aren't for you. On the other hand, if you're someone who wants to eat less meat and is sick of pasta with tomato sauce and Parmesan cheese, read on. I think this will be the beginning of a beautiful relationship!

One of the things I found most interesting about writing a vegetarian noodle book is that when I began to tell people about it no one thought it was odd. There I was, a lactating mother, a classically trained chef and the daughter of a beef farmer, and I was confessing to cooking meatless noodle recipes for months on end. It just goes to show you that opinions about vegetarianism have changed a lot in the recent past.

In the good old days when meat, potatoes and two veg reigned over the North American dinner table, vegetarians were the weird neighbors down the street who listened to sitar music and slouched around the block looking pale and wan in their Birkenstock sandals. Today's vegetarians are harder to spot; they're wearing cross-trainers, patent leather pumps, army boots and even Gucci slip-ons. For in the quarter century since Frances Moore Lappé wrote her breakthrough vegetarian book *Diet for a Small Planet,* our society's views regarding diet and health have changed significantly. We've become conscious eaters who care not only about how the food we eat tastes but about how it affects our well-being.

This awareness, coupled with our increased exposure to foods from other cultures, has spawned a new type of vegetarian – the occasional vegetarian – who eats meatless or virtually meatless meals the majority of the time, saving meat for celebrations and special occasions. The concept of the occasional vegetarian is new only in Western society. In the Orient and India (regions whose cuisines heavily influence the recipes in this book) low-meat and virtually meatless diets have been the norm for centuries. Tellingly, such cultures also have lower obesity, cancer and heart disease rates than North America and Europe.

My recipes are born not only of my love for noodles but out of my love for distinctive flavors, easy preparation and novelty. You won't find many mainstream pasta recipes in this book unless I've come up with a way to make it faster and better. Such is the case with Quick Skillet Macaroni and Cheese (page 64), which is one of the best and easiest mac & cheese recipes I've ever seen. What you will find on these pages are recipes that suit the lifestyles of people who, like me, are on the run and want to eat in a rush without sacrificing taste, quality or well-being.

I'm trained as a chef and have earned my living as a cookery writer for a long time, but several things about cooking noodles at home still surprised me:

1. Many of the exotic-sounding ingredients I needed were easy to get at my local supermarket;

2. It was so much faster to throw together a quick, nutritious noodle supper than to cook a frozen store-bought concoction that I didn't really enjoy; and

3. I became slim and trim again while eating food I really liked.

I hope as you go through this collection of fast and easy noodle dishes that you will find eating noodles just as satisfying and enjoyable as I do.

# WHAT IS TIME?

Time is precious. That's what it is and if you're like me or anyone I know, you rarely have enough of it or can afford to waste it by doing something you don't enjoy. That's why I've arranged this book the way I have. The simplest recipes are at the front in a section I've dubbed "15-Minute Recipes." As you'd expect, these recipes take 15 minutes or less to prepare, from the time you've assembled your raw ingredients, if you're a cook with average knife skills, good organizational skills and rudimentary cooking knowledge. In fact, some of these dishes are so easy to make it may take you longer to read the recipe and assemble the ingredients than to prepare the food! A word of advice: since the cooking time for these dishes is so minimal, prepare all your ingredients for each recipe before you put anything on the stove. You don't want to be chopping your garlic when you should be cooking it.

To create such quick and easy recipes I have suggested a few compromises along the way, like using bought curry mixes, canned cooked beans and frozen ingredients such as cooked spinach or Asian vegetable mixes. Wherever possible I've tried to help fledgling cooks learn about organizing themselves as they cook by using the word "meanwhile" as a key to tasks that can be done while something else does its thing. You'll also find throughout the text information about unusual ingredients and substitutes that might be more available to you.

"30 Minute Recipes" and "45 Minute Recipes" are for evenings when you have a little more time but still don't want to make a career out of being in the kitchen. Together, the 45-minute and 30-minute recipes take up about half of the book, so you see my emphasis is on the faster, easier fare.

Although some of the recipes in *Noodles Express* cook in less time than specified, you should schedule for preparation and cooking to sometimes require an extra few minutes here and there – especially given that everyone's preparation skills vary and that it's inevitable telephones will ring or children will cry as soon as you're busy chopping.

All that said, let's not waste any more time. Let's get cooking!

# FIVE THINGS YOU SHOULD KNOW

**1.** Many of these recipes are low in fat but certainly not all of them are lean. However, the absence of meat in every recipe means that even when the ingredients sound and taste rich, you can afford to eat them a little more often than when the same things are paired with meat. I don't like the taste and textures of low-fat sour cream, cheeses or mayonnaise; I'd rather eat less of a really good thing than a lot of an okay thing. But if you would like to substitute low-fat products for the full-fat ones I call for, please go ahead. In all cases, except for where my recipes call for reducing whipping cream, using lower-fat versions of what the recipe calls for will not ruin the recipe.

**2.** Like most people, I have a very busy life, but I'd still rather cook my own fresh food than rely on prepared convenience products. Having said that, you'll see that in this book I do call for products that can help you to cook dinner in a hurry. For instance, frozen chopped vegetables, curry pastes and canned tomatoes are items I always keep on hand since they make it much easier to prepare a fresh hot meal on a busy weeknight. The way I see it, if your alternative is dinner from the drive-through window, then a few frozen vegetables can be endured!

**3.** I don't claim that the recipes in this book are definitive or classical; instead, they are concoctions I devised from the ingredients offered at an average supermarket. Likewise, these dishes are the creations of an average gal. I didn't travel the world (or even a small part of it) to source out authentic or regional noodle combinations. On the contrary, these recipes are a personal collection of foods I like to eat; they use fairly easy-to-find ingredients and make compromises whenever convenience can be accommodated without sacrificing quality.

You'll notice, by the way, that I use Tabasco sauce in my recipes. I'm aware of the many other brands of hot pepper sauce on the market. The variance in their taste and heat intensity is great, though, so I prefer to call for a product I know works in my recipes. But if you have a favorite other sauce, by all means, go ahead and experiment.

**4.** Because I'm not a vegetarian, I almost always use lean chicken stock when I make these (or any other) recipes. I like the viscosity chicken stock gives to a sauce and the depth of flavor it adds to the overall dish. I have, however, made sure that these recipes work with all kinds of stock. Recipe tester Beatrice Damore and I experimented with home-made varieties of chicken and vegetable stock, frozen deli varieties of fish, meat and vegetable stocks, and all the powdered and canned stuff to be found on the grocer's shelves. Although overall flavors and the thickness of sauces varied slightly depending on which type of stock we used, we concluded that when used correctly, an acceptable result can be achieved with any of these products.

**5.** Some points to keep in mind if you decide to cook with bought stock are that commercial varieties of meat or vegetable stock can be very salty, so hold back on adding any salt the recipe may call for until you've tasted the completed dish. Also, did you know that powdered stocks and cubes, regardless of the flavor they impart, are vegetarian? According to McCormick's Canada, you can have the depth of flavor that beef or chicken stock add to dishes without eating any meat if you use bouillon cubes. So, if you're a vegetarian who isn't grossed out by the taste of meat, you can safely use any stock cubes without compromising your principles . . . much.

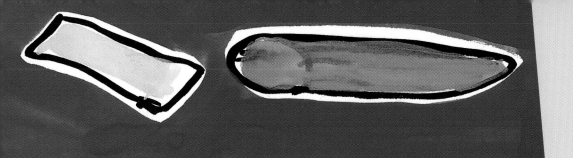

# Noodles, Noodles, Noodles!

# ABOUT NOODLES

In each recipe I've called for a specific type of noodle and, in some cases, a second-best substitute. I know that in some places, especially smaller towns, the selection of Asian noodles and even semolina pasta can be meager. If you have trouble finding a specific type of noodle don't give up on making a recipe. Instead, try to find a noodle that shares some of the characteristics of the hard-to-find noodle. To help you, here's a description of some of the less familiar noodles I've used in this book.

**Bean starch noodles:** these translucent, whitish noodles look like rice noodles and are inter-changeable with rice noodles in the recipes in this book.

**Bucatini:** a long hollow semolina pasta that is just a bit thicker than spaghetti.

**Chow mein:** like Italian noodles, chow mein noodles are made from a mixture of eggs, wheat flour and water. They are extruded into long noodles of varying widths and are usually sold fresh or pre-cooked in vacuum packages; good-quality dry varieties are available in some markets.

**Ditali:** very short tubular semolina pasta.

**Radiatore:** these radiator-shaped noodles have lots of nooks and crannies to hold sauce well.

**Ramen:** the most popular noodle in Japan, these instant noodles are widely available. Sold in little dehydrated bricks, ramen cook quickly in broth; these long, thin noodles are pale yellow and have a pretty crimped texture when dry.

**Rice noodles:** available dried and imported from many countries. The packaging of these noodles is inconsistent, so forgive me if what one of my recipes calls for doesn't match what you find at your market. All rice noodles cook very quickly, so if you're unsure about whether you are using exactly what my recipe calls for, err on the side of caution and test for doneness before the time I've specified for cooking or soaking elapses.

**Skoo-bi-do:** a semolina pasta shaped like a loose corkscrew and tubular like elbow macaroni.

**Soba:** a specialty of northern Japan, these slender noodles are made from buckwheat flour (some brands may contain a mixture of buckwheat and wheat flour); they have a very appealing, nutty flavor and a pleasant toothsome texture. Soba noodles contain protein, vitamins $B^1$ and $B^2$, calcium and iron, all nutrients that are often lacking in vegetarian diets. Soba are most readily available frozen in vacuum-sealed packages in the deli section. The dry variety of these noodles has a vastly superior texture but is hard to find. If Korean naeng myun noodles are sold at your store, they are a great substitute for soba.

**Udon:** wheat noodles that are long and cylindrical; they are sold fresh in vacuum packages in the refrigerator section of grocery stores. When cooked they have a slick exterior finish and a chewy, somewhat stodgy texture. Fettuccine and linguine are both good substitutes.

# 15
# Minutes

# Hot and Sour Soup and Noodle Supper

All you need to make a terrific light meal is a bowl of this hot and sour noodle soup and some crusty bread. The tantalizing combination of flavors in this soup makes it irresistible.

| | |
|---|---|
| 4 cups | vegetable or chicken stock |
| 1 | dried wood ear or other mushroom |
| 2 tbsp | tamari |
| 1 tbsp | minced gingerroot |
| 1 tbsp | rice vinegar |
| 1 tsp | granulated sugar |
| 1 tsp | sambal oelek or Tabasco sauce |
| 1/2 tsp | toasted sesame oil |
| 2 oz | rice stick noodles |
| 4 oz | silken tofu |
| 2 | green onions, sliced |

- **Heat** 1 cup of the stock and pour over wood ear; let soak for 10 minutes or until softened. Drain, reserving stock, and slice mushroom as thinly as possible.

- **Meanwhile**, in saucepan set over medium-high heat, combine remaining stock, tamari, ginger, vinegar, sugar, sambal oelek and sesame oil. Bring to a boil. Taste and adjust seasoning if necessary.

- **Rinse** noodles under running water; shake off excess moisture and add to pot; simmer for 2 minutes. Meanwhile, finely dice tofu. Stir wood ears, soaking liquid, tofu and green onions into soup; cook for 1 minute or until piping hot.

*Makes 4 servings.*

STIR

**Make-Ahead Tip:** Can be made, up to point of adding green onions, up to 2 days ahead. Add green onions when reheating.

**Tamari:** True Japanese tamari is rich and dark with a slightly sweet flavor. Unlike soy sauce, which contains wheat, tamari is starch free. However, some North American brands use the term "tamari" to denote any Japanese-style soy sauce, so if you have a wheat allergy, check the ingredients list to be sure that the tamari is wheat free.

# Fresh Pea and Egg Noodle Soup

What could be more evocative of springtime than tiny sweet peas? This soup is fresh and mild – a sure hit with kids!

| | |
|---|---|
| 1 tbsp | butter |
| 1/2 cup | sliced leeks, white part only, or onion |
| 1/4 tsp | each salt and pepper |
| pinch | granulated sugar |
| 6 cups | vegetable stock |
| 3 | fine egg noodle nests (3 oz each) |
| 1 cup | fresh or thawed frozen tiny peas |
| 1 cup | shredded Napa cabbage |
| 2 tbsp | chopped fresh chervil or parsley |

■ **In large** saucepan set over medium heat, melt butter; add leeks, salt, pepper and sugar. Cook, stirring, for 5 minutes or until softened.

■ **Add** stock and bring to a boil. Add pasta nests and boil for 5 minutes or until nests have broken apart and are almost al dente.

■ **Add** peas, cabbage and chervil; cover and boil for 2 minutes or until peas are bright green and tender.

*Makes 4 servings.*

# FIVE-MINUTE TOMATO RAMEN SOUP

In Japan, ramen noodles are the equivalent of the cheese and crackers we snack on in North America; the Japanese stop in at noodle houses for a ramen noodle break whenever they need a little pick-me-up.

| | |
|---|---|
| 2 cups | vegetable stock |
| 2 cups | V8 or **Clamato** juice |
| 1 tbsp | pickled ginger juice |
| 2 cups | shredded **spinach** leaves |
| 1 tbsp | soy sauce |
| 1 | pkg. (3 oz/85 g) **ramen** noodles, flavor sachet discarded |
| 1 cup | frozen **tiny peas** |
| 2 | green onions, chopped |

■ **In saucepan** set over medium-high heat, bring stock, V8 juice and pickled ginger juice to a boil. Stir in spinach and soy sauce; return to boil. Stir in noodles and peas; return to boil and cook for 2 minutes or until noodles are tender. Stir in green onions.

*Makes 4 servings.*

**Ramen Noodles:** Although native to China, ramen noodles are most popular in Japan. They are those delicious, inexpensive crinkled-up noodles that are sold in square packages. Ramen noodles take only a few minutes to cook and are most often served as a noodle stew in rich, hearty broth.

# Zippy Ramen

I've named this dish "Zippy" because these noodles are fast to make as well as spicy.

In true noodle houses you see people happily slurping their ramen noodles to oxygenate the flavors and make each bowl of soup a sight, sound, smell and taste experience. Maybe that's why noodle houses often seat diners at stools that face the wall!

| | |
|---|---|
| 1 tbsp | chili oil |
| 1 | small onion, thinly sliced |
| 1 | clove garlic, minced |
| 1 tbsp | chili-ginger sauce |
| 1 tbsp | soy sauce |
| 4 cups | vegetable or chicken stock |
| 2 cups | frozen Asian-style vegetables |
| 1 | pkg. (3 oz/85 g) ramen noodles, flavor sachet discarded |
| 2 | green onions, sliced |

■ **Heat oil** in large saucepan set over medium heat; add onion and cook, stirring often, for 5 minutes. Add garlic, chili-ginger sauce and soy sauce; cook for 1 minute.

■ **Stir in stock** and bring to a boil. Stir in vegetables and return to boil. Add noodles and bring back to boil; cook for 2 minutes. Ladle soup into bowls and sprinkle with green onions.

*Makes 4 servings.*

# MUSHROOM AND NOODLE SNACK IN LEMON BROTH

**Because of the butter used to sauté the mushrooms, this recipe has an unctuous, satisfying quality that makes it a real winner on a cold day.**

| | |
|---|---|
| 1 tbsp | butter |
| 1 cup | sliced **shiitake** or button mushrooms |
| 4 cups | vegetable **stock** |
| 1 tbsp | chili-ginger sauce |
| 1 | stalk **lemongrass**, chopped |
| 1 | pkg. (3 oz/85 g) **ramen** noodles, flavor sachet discarded |
| 1/4 cup | chopped **chives** or green onions |
| | Salt and pepper |

■ **Melt** butter in large saucepan set over high heat; add mushrooms and cook, stirring often, for 5 to 7 minutes or until well browned; remove from pan and reserve.

■ **Stir** in stock, chili-ginger sauce and lemongrass. Bring to a boil; reduce heat and simmer for 5 minutes. Using a slotted spoon, remove as much of the lemongrass as possible and discard. Stir in mushrooms and noodles; bring to a boil and cook for 2 minutes. Remove from heat and stir in chives. Taste and adjust seasoning if necessary.

*Makes 4 servings.*

**Note on Lemongrass:** Recipe tester Beatrice Damore and I came to the conclusion that bottled, powdered and preserved lemongrass were not worth buying. Dried stalks will work well in this recipe, but no other substitute for fresh lemongrass is recommended.

# Spoon and Fork Asian Noodle Soup

This easy dish is great for dinners or lunches when you want something satisfying but don't have time to prepare a full meal.

| | |
|---|---|
| 4 cups | vegetable or chicken **stock** |
| 1 1/2 tbsp | light soy sauce |
| 1 tsp | grated gingerroot |
| 1/4 tsp | Tabasco sauce |
| 2 | cloves garlic, halved |
| 2 | green onions, thinly sliced |
| 1 cup | **snow peas** |
| 1 | small **red pepper** |
| 1 | pkg. (3 oz/85 g) **ramen** noodles, flavor sachet discarded |
| | Fresh coriander leaves for garnish |

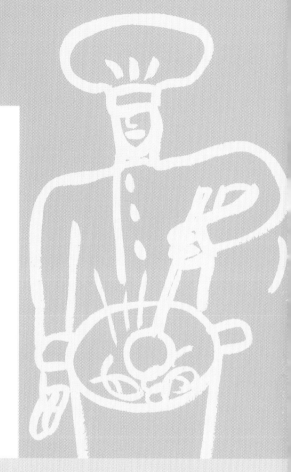

■ **In saucepan** set over medium-high heat, bring stock to a boil. Add soy sauce, ginger, Tabasco, garlic and half the green onions; return to boil and simmer for 5 minutes. Discard garlic halves.

■ **Meanwhile**, remove stem end from snow peas and halve diagonally. Cut red pepper into large chunks. Add vegetables to boiling stock and cook for 3 minutes or until peppers are becoming tender. Stir in noodles and cook for 1 minute longer. Ladle soup into bowls and sprinkle with remaining green onions and coriander leaves.

*Makes 4 servings.*

**Soy Sauce:** Soy sauce is made by combining roasted soybeans, wheat, yeast, brine and a bacteria culture. The mixture is then aged for up to two years before being strained and bottled.

Soy sauce comes in dark and light varieties, the light sauce being aged for a shorter time than the dark. I prefer the flavor of light soy sauce; however, if you have only dark on hand it too will work well in my recipes as long as you use a light touch.

# NOODLES IN MUSHROOM GINGER BROTH

You can use any noodles – fresh or dry – that are on hand for this easy soup. I like it with linguine, which is toothsome and stands up well against the mushrooms.

| | |
|---|---|
| 4 | dried shiitake or other mushrooms |
| 1 | dried wood ear mushroom |
| 4 cups | hot vegetable or chicken stock |
| 1 tsp | each toasted sesame oil and vegetable oil |
| 2 | cloves garlic, minced |
| 1 tbsp | minced gingerroot |
| 1 tsp | chili sauce or ketchup |
| 1 tsp | light soy sauce |
| 1 cup | cooked linguine (about 3 oz dried) |
| | Fresh coriander leaves for garnish |

■ **Place** mushrooms in large bowl and pour over hot stock; let stand for 10 minutes or until mushrooms are softened.

■ **Meanwhile**, heat sesame oil and vegetable oil in large saucepan set over medium-low heat; add garlic and ginger and cook, stirring often, for 5 minutes or until garlic is translucent.

■ **Stir in** chili sauce and soy sauce. Increase heat to high. Pour mushroom liquid through a fine sieve into pan and mix well. Chop shiitake mushrooms into strips and wood ear into very thin strips; add mushrooms and noodles to pan and cook for 3 minutes or until heated through. Ladle into heated bowls and garnish with coriander leaves.

*Makes 4 servings.*

**Wood Ear Mushrooms:** Also called cloud ears, tree ears or black mushrooms, these curled, tough mushrooms are a good source of iron and have long been used to add texture and to carry flavors through many Indonesian, Malaysian, Thai and Chinese dishes. In fact, documented use of wood ears in cooking exists in China as early as the Tang dynasty (618–907 AD).

# GREEN CURRY AND GREEN APPLE SALAD

My detractors will definitely shout "Fusion runs amok!" when they see this recipe. But wacky as it sounds, this combination is really delicious and will spice up any picnic or outdoor meal.

| | |
|---|---|
| 2 cups | tri-color penne |
| 1 cup | mayonnaise |
| 1/2 cup | sour cream or yogurt |
| 1 tbsp | Thai green curry paste |
| 1 cup | finely chopped celery |
| 1 cup | shredded unpeeled green apple |
| 1/4 cup | chopped fresh parsley |

■ **In pot** of boiling salted water, cook pasta for 8 to 10 minutes or until al dente. Drain and refresh under cold water; drain well and reserve.

■ **In large bowl**, stir together mayonnaise, sour cream and curry paste until fully mixed. Stir in pasta, celery, apple and parsley until well combined. Taste and adjust seasoning if necessary.

*Makes 4 to 6 servings.*

**Thai Green Curry Paste:** One of the most popular Thai curry mixtures, green curry contains lots of herbs and green chilies. It is traditionally used to make a soupy coconut milk sauce for rice or noodles.

The challenge to making homemade curry paste lies in finding the fresh ingredients. Hard-to-find galangal, kaffir lime leaves, young green lemongrass and superlative hot green chilies are absolutely essential to get the right balance of flavors. Fortunately, several brands of fairly good curry paste are available today for international but time-challenged cooks like you and me.

# RED CURRY BROTH WITH OODLES OF NOODLES

To make a true red curry, you need galangal, kaffir lime leaves and fresh young lemongrass – all ingredients that are difficult to find in most mainstream supermarkets. More and more often, though, red curry paste mixes are available in shops. Here's how they can be used to make a fast, delicious bowl of noodles.

| | |
|---|---|
| 3 oz | pre-cooked chow mein noodles (about ¼ pkg.) |
| 3 tbsp | vegetable oil |
| 2 tsp | Thai red curry paste |
| 8 oz | firm tofu, cubed |
| 1 cup | each chopped green and yellow beans |
| 4 cups | vegetable stock |
| 1 tbsp | tamari or light soy sauce |
| ¼ cup | chopped fresh coriander |

■ **Loosen noodles** with your fingers; immerse in boiling water for 1 minute. Drain well and reserve.

■ **Heat half** the oil in wok or large deep skillet set over medium-high heat. Stir in curry paste and cook, stirring, for 1 minute or until very fragrant. Stir in tofu and stir-fry for 2 minutes; remove from pan and reserve.

■ **Add remaining oil** to pan. Add green and yellow beans and stir-fry for 1 minute. Add stock and tamari and bring to a boil; cover and cook for 2 minutes or until beans are almost tender. Stir in tofu, noodles and coriander and return to boil.

*Makes 4 servings.*

# Chow Mein Salad with Citrus Dressing

This salad is as great looking as it is tasty! Make it any time you want to serve a salad that's a little different but will still appeal to everyone.

| | |
|---|---|
| 12 oz | pre-cooked chow mein noodles, or 4 cups cooked spaghetti |
| 1/4 cup | toasted sesame oil |
| 1/2 cup | thinly sliced matchstick-length pieces of carrot |
| 1 cup | thinly sliced snow peas |
| 1/2 cup | thinly sliced matchstick-length pieces of daikon or red radish |
| 1/4 cup | fresh coriander leaves |
| 1/4 cup | orange juice |
| 3 tbsp | tamari |
| 1 tbsp | grated gingerroot |
| 1 1/2 tbsp | rice vinegar |
| 1 1/2 tbsp | cider vinegar |
| 2 tsp | granulated sugar |
| 1/2 tsp | long thin pieces of orange zest |
| 1/4 tsp | Tabasco sauce |
| 1/4 cup | chopped toasted peanuts (see page 76) |

■ **Gently** loosen noodles with your fingers. Immerse noodles in boiling water for 1 minute. Drain well; fluff with a fork and toss with 1 tsp of the sesame oil. Reserve.

■ **In saucepan** of boiling salted water, cook carrots for 2 minutes; add snow peas and cook for 1 minute longer. Drain and rinse under cold running water until cool. Drain well and add to noodles; mix in daikon and coriander.

■ **In small** bowl or measuring cup, combine orange juice, tamari, ginger, rice vinegar, cider vinegar, sugar, orange zest and Tabasco sauce. Whisking constantly, drizzle in remaining sesame oil. Pour over noodle mixture and toss to combine. Sprinkle with peanuts.

*Makes 4 to 6 servings.*

**Make-Ahead Tip:** Use only half the dressing at first. Just before serving, toss the salad with the remaining dressing.

**Daikon:** This long smooth white radish is terrifically crunchy and fresh tasting. It contains twice as much vitamin C as red radishes. In some supermarkets daikon is sold as mooli or loh bak.

# PAINTED DESERT PASTA SALAD

Here I've combined the great flavors of the Southwest to make a pasta salad that is packed full of fiber, vegetable protein and goodness.

| | |
|---|---|
| 8 oz | tri-color pasta shells |
| 1 1/2 cups | cooked black beans |
| 1/2 | each red and orange pepper, chopped |
| 1/2 cup | thinly sliced red onion |
| 2 tbsp | lime juice |
| 1 tbsp | chili powder |
| 1 tbsp | cider vinegar |
| 1 tsp | liquid honey |
| 1 | clove garlic, minced |
| 1/2 tsp | each salt and pepper |
| 1/2 cup | extra virgin olive oil |
| 1 cup | chopped avocado |
| 2 tbsp | chopped fresh coriander |

■ **In large** pot of boiling salted water, cook pasta for 8 to 10 minutes or until al dente. Drain and rinse under cold water; drain well. Stir in black beans, red and orange peppers and onion.

■ **In small** bowl or measuring cup, whisk together lime juice, chili powder, vinegar, honey, garlic, salt and pepper. Whisking constantly, drizzle in oil until well combined.

■ **Pour over** noodle mixture and stir until well combined. Gently stir in avocado and coriander. Taste and adjust seasoning if necessary.

*Makes 6 to 8 servings.*

**Avocados:** Although this fruit is rich in oil and calories, it also contains lots of vitamins. To choose an avocado, look for a clear, unblemished skin that yields to slight pressure at the stem end. Hard avocados will ripen in a day or two if stored at room temperature.

# ZESTY PASTA SALAD WITH PEPPERY GREENS

This is a great outdoor-weather salad, especially when served with grilled vegetables and baked potatoes.

| | |
|---|---|
| 12 oz | bucatini or linguine |
| 1 tsp | olive oil |
| 1 1/2 cups | shredded radicchio |
| 1 cup | packed arugula leaves |
| 1 | yellow pepper, thinly sliced |

## DRESSING

| | |
|---|---|
| 2 tbsp | aged balsamic vinegar |
| 1 tsp | dried thyme |
| 1 tsp | black pepper |
| 3/4 tsp | salt |
| 4 | cloves garlic, minced |
| 2 | oil-packed sun-dried tomatoes |
| 2/3 cup | extra virgin olive oil |
| 1/4 cup | chopped fresh basil |

■ **To make** dressing, in small bowl, mix together balsamic vinegar, thyme, pepper, salt and garlic. Finely chop tomatoes and add to dressing. Whisking constantly, drizzle in 2/3 cup extra virgin olive oil until well combined. Stir in basil.

■ **In large** pot of boiling salted water, cook pasta for 8 to 10 minutes or until al dente. Drain well; toss with 1 tsp olive oil. Let cool to room temperature. Toss with radicchio, arugula and yellow pepper. Drizzle dressing over salad and toss until well combined. Taste and adjust seasoning if necessary.

*Makes 4 servings.*

**Variation**
**Goat Cheese–Almond Pasta Salad:** For a full meal in a bowl, top salad with 2 oz crumbled goat cheese and 1/4 cup toasted slivered almonds (see page 76).

# Soba Salad with Tamari Dressing and Broccoli

**Soba noodles have a nice nutty flavor that adds depth to this yummy salad.**

| | |
|---|---|
| 1 | pkg. (12 oz/350 g) pre-cooked **soba** noodles, or 4 cups cooked whole wheat spaghetti |
| 1/4 cup | **tamari** |
| 2 tbsp | grated gingerroot |
| 2 tbsp | **lime** juice |
| 1 tsp | **Tabasco** sauce |
| 1/2 tsp | brown sugar |
| 2 tbsp | toasted sesame oil |
| 1/4 cup | vegetable oil |
| 3 cups | finely chopped cooked **broccoli** |
| 2 | plum **tomatoes**, seeded and chopped |
| 1/3 cup | toasted whole blanched **almonds** (see page 76) |

■ **Loosen noodles** with your fingers. Place in large bowl and cover with boiling water; let stand for 2 to 3 minutes. Drain well; fluff with a fork and reserve.

■ **In large bowl**, whisk together tamari, ginger, lime juice, Tabasco sauce and brown sugar. Whisking constantly, slowly drizzle in sesame and vegetable oils.

■ **Add broccoli** and tomatoes and toss to coat in dressing. Add noodles and almonds; using two spoons, gently toss to combine. Taste and adjust seasoning.

*Makes 4 servings.*

**The Low-Down on Soba:** Many North American supermarkets car vacuum-sealed packages of pre-cooked soba noodles in their refrig erator section. Noodles sold this way are a good product to use in these recipes, but note the expiration date because they don't last long as other pre-cooked noodles.

I've experimented with dried and frozen pre-cooked soba. The dried noodles are expensive and difficult to find but have a superio taste and texture. Frozen noodles are often terribly gluey and fall apart. If frozen is the only variety you can find, use whole wheat spaghetti instead.

# CAMPFIRE SWEET POTATO AND PASTA SALAD

**If you're craving the taste of the outdoors, then look no further. This high-fiber salad has all the taste of life on the range.**

| | |
|---|---|
| 1/2 lb | **sweet potatoes** (about 1 large) |
| 4 oz | pasta **shells** or elbow macaroni |
| 1/2 cup | mayonnaise |
| 2 tsp | **smoky Dijon** mustard, or 2 tsp Dijon plus 1/2 tsp natural hickory liquid smoke |
| 1 tsp | **chili** powder |
| 1/4 tsp | each ground cumin and dried oregano leaves |
| 1/4 tsp | pepper |
| 4 | **radishes**, halved and thinly sliced |
| 2 | green onions, chopped |
| 2 cups | lightly packed chopped **watercress** |

■ **Peel** sweet potatoes and cut into chunks. Place in pot of cold salted water and bring to a boil; reduce heat to medium and simmer for 6 minutes or until fork-tender. Drain and cool to room temperature.

■ **Cook** pasta in large pot of boiling salted water for 8 to 10 minutes or until al dente. Drain well and reserve.

■ **In large** bowl, stir together mayonnaise, mustard, chili powder, cumin, oregano and pepper. Gently stir in potatoes, pasta, radishes and green onions. Just before serving, stir in watercress.

*Makes 4 servings.*

**Tip:** If you're watching your fat intake, substitute light mayonnaise.

# Penne, Asparagus and Yellow Peppers with Champagne-Saffron Vinaigrette

Asparagus is usually plentiful and inexpensive in springtime, which means that this colorful salad is a fabulous choice for an Easter buffet or a springtime brunch.

| | |
|---|---|
| 12 oz | penne |
| 1 cup | asparagus tips |
| pinch | saffron threads |
| 1 tbsp | champagne vinegar or white wine vinegar |
| 1/2 tsp | granulated sugar |
| 1/2 tsp | each salt and pepper |
| 1/2 tsp | Dijon mustard |
| 1/3 cup | extra virgin olive oil |
| 1/4 cup | chopped fresh basil |
| 1 | yellow pepper, chopped |
| | Lettuce leaves |

■ **In a pot** of boiling salted water, cook pasta for 5 minutes; add asparagus and cook for 4 minutes or until asparagus is tender and pasta is al dente. Drain and run under cold water until completely cooled; drain well.

■ **Meanwhile**, rub saffron threads between fingers and sprinkle into a large bowl. Stir in 1 tsp very hot water. Let stand for 2 minutes or until softened. Stir in vinegar, sugar, salt, pepper and mustard. Whisking constantly, drizzle in olive oil. Stir in basil, pasta, asparagus and yellow pepper; toss to coat. Taste and adjust seasoning if necessary. Spoon into a shallow bowl lined with lettuce leaves.

*Makes 4 to 6 servings.*

# TORTELLINI SALAD À LA GRECQUE

My longtime vegetarian friend Laura Baehr introduced me to this salad years ago. Although tortellini and Greece don't usually go together, here the flavors and textures of a Greek salad make a crunchy match with cheese-filled tortellini.

| | |
|---|---|
| 1 tbsp | chopped fresh oregano (or 1 tsp dried) |
| 1 tbsp | white wine vinegar |
| 1 tsp | lemon juice |
| 1 tsp | anchovy paste |
| 1 | clove garlic, minced |
| 1/4 tsp | each salt and pepper |
| pinch | granulated sugar |
| 1/2 cup | extra virgin olive oil |
| 12 oz | fresh small cheese-filled tortellini noodles |
| 1 | plum tomato, seeded and chopped |
| 1/2 | red onion, thinly sliced |
| 1/2 cup | chopped English cucumber |
| 1/2 cup | pitted halved Kalamata olives |
| 1/4 cup | chopped fresh parsley |
| 1/4 cup | crumbled feta cheese |

■ **In small** bowl whisk together oregano, vinegar, lemon juice, anchovy paste, garlic, salt, pepper and sugar. Whisking constantly, drizzle in olive oil in a slow steady stream; whisk until well combined. (Dressing keeps in refrigerator for up to 2 days.)

■ **In large** pot of boiling salted water, cook noodles for 3 to 5 minutes or until floating and tender. Drain and rinse under cold water. Drain well. Transfer to large bowl and toss with 1 tbsp of the dressing.

■ **Stir** tomato, onion, cucumber, olives and parsley into noodles; drizzle dressing over top and stir until well coated. Taste and adjust seasoning if necessary. Sprinkle with feta cheese.

*Makes 4 servings.*

# Orange-Infused Beet and Orecchiette Salad

This salad is a real knock-out when it comes to both looks and flavor. You can use canned beets, but home-cooked ones will give you the best results.

| | |
|---|---|
| 6 oz | orecchiette or other short pasta |
| 4 | cooked beets |
| 1 tbsp | orange zest |
| 1/4 cup | orange juice |
| 1 tbsp | finely chopped shallot or onion |
| 1 1/2 tsp | white wine vinegar |
| 1/2 tsp | granulated sugar |
| 1 | small clove garlic, minced |
| 1 tsp | grainy mustard |
| 1/4 cup | extra virgin olive oil |
| 1/4 cup | coarsely chopped toasted hazelnuts (see page 76) |
| 2 tbsp | chopped chives |

■ **In large** pot of boiling salted water, cook pasta for 8 to 10 minutes or until al dente; drain well. Chop beets into bite-sized pieces and toss with pasta. Stir in orange zest.

■ **In small** saucepan set over medium-high heat, bring orange juice, shallot, vinegar, sugar and garlic to a boil. Simmer for 1 to 2 minutes or until reduced and syrupy. Stir in mustard. Whisking constantly, drizzle in olive oil. Pour over beet mixture and stir until well combined. Just before serving, stir in hazelnuts and chives.

*Makes 4 servings.*

**To Cook Beets:** Freshly cooked beets offer unsurpassed taste and color over canned varieties. Depending on your schedule, either of the following methods can be used to prepare fresh beets.

1. Oven roasting provides the best flavor and color and retains the most nutrients. Place washed beets in baking pan; cover tightly with foil and bake in 375°F oven for about 1 hour. The skins will slip right off the cooked beets.

2. Microwave braising does leech some of the color from beets but it's fast and easy. Cut beets into uniform pieces and place in a casserole dish. Add 1/4 cup water. Cover tightly and cook on High power for 8 to 10 minutes or until fork-tender. Slip off skins.

# CURRIED ORZO SALAD

Here's the perfect salad for curry novices and aficionados alike. In this recipe the curry works as a subdued base so that all the flavors have a chance to sing.

| | |
|---|---|
| 1/3 cup | olive oil |
| 1 tbsp | **mild curry** paste |
| 2 tsp | minced **gingerroot** |
| 1 tbsp | rice vinegar |
| 2 tsp | lime juice |
| 1/2 tsp | finely chopped **lime** zest |
| 3 tbsp | each chopped fresh parsley and **chives** |
| 2 1/2 cups | **orzo** |
| 1/3 cup | **currants** |
| 2 tbsp | dry sherry, heated |
| 2 tbsp | chopped toasted almonds (see page 76) |
| | Salt and pepper to taste |

■ **In small** saucepan set over medium heat, stir together oil, curry paste and ginger. Heat until ginger just begins to sizzle. Remove from heat and let stand for 5 minutes. Whisk in vinegar, lime juice, lime zest, parsley and chives. (Dressing may be prepared to this point up to 2 days ahead.)

■ **In pot** of boiling salted water, cook orzo for 6 to 7 minutes or until tender but not mushy. Drain and cool under cold running water; drain well and transfer to large bowl.

■ **Meanwhile**, stir together currants and sherry; let stand for 5 minutes. Add currants, sherry and dressing to orzo and toss to combine well. Season with salt and pepper to taste. Up to 15 minutes before serving, stir in almonds.

*Makes 4 servings.*

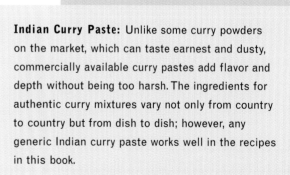

heat oil

**Indian Curry Paste:** Unlike some curry powders on the market, which can taste earnest and dusty, commercially available curry pastes add flavor and depth without being too harsh. The ingredients for authentic curry mixtures vary not only from country to country but from dish to dish; however, any generic Indian curry paste works well in the recipes in this book.

# MACARONI AND LENTIL SALAD

If you're an athlete, a pregnant or lactating woman or you just love the exotic flavors of North Africa, then this salad is for you. This delicious combination of pasta, lentils and dried fruit provides lots of fiber and protein to keep your body in peak condition.

| | |
|---|---|
| 1 tbsp | cider vinegar |
| 1 tsp | mild curry paste |
| 1 tsp | Dijon mustard |
| 3/4 tsp | each salt and pepper |
| 1/4 tsp | each cinnamon, nutmeg, ground cardamom and granulated sugar |
| pinch | ground cloves |
| 1/2 cup | extra virgin olive oil |
| 4 oz | elbow macaroni |
| 1 cup | cooked brown lentils |
| 3/4 cup | finely chopped English cucumber |
| 1/4 cup | chopped dried apricots |
| 1/4 cup | chopped fresh parsley |
| 3 | plum tomatoes, seeded and chopped |
| 2 | green onions, chopped |

■ **In large** bowl, whisk together vinegar, curry paste, mustard, salt, pepper, cinnamon, nutmeg, cardamom, sugar and cloves. Whisking constantly, drizzle in oil until well combined.

■ **In large** pot of boiling salted water, cook pasta for 8 to 10 minutes or until al dente. Drain well. Add pasta to dressing and stir to coat well.

■ **Add** lentils, cucumber, apricots, parsley, tomatoes and green onions; stir gently to combine. Taste and adjust seasoning if necessary.

*Makes 4 servings.*

**Tip:** Although cooked lentils are available frozen, cooking your own is simple. Bring 1/2 cup rinsed dried lentils to a boil in 2 cups water; reduce heat to low, cover and simmer for 35 to 40 minutes or until tender. Drain and rinse well.

# CREAMY WASABI PASTA AND RED BEAN SALAD

The combination of kidney beans and pasta makes this a healthy full-meal salad for hot weather – or any time you want something fresh tasting.

| | |
|---|---|
| 6 oz | tri-color fusilli or farfalle |
| 1 1/2 tbsp | wasabi powder |
| 1 tbsp | mirin or medium sherry |
| 3/4 cup | mayonnaise |
| 1/4 cup | yogurt or sour cream |
| 1 | clove garlic, minced |
| 1/4 cup | finely chopped fresh coriander |
| 1/2 tsp | each salt and pepper |
| 2 | plum tomatoes |
| 1 cup | cooked red kidney beans |
| 1/4 cup | chopped daikon or radishes |

▪ **In large** pot of boiling salted water, cook pasta for 8 to 10 minutes or until al dente. Drain and rinse under cold running water; drain well. Reserve in large bowl.

▪ **In small** bowl, dissolve wasabi powder in mirin. Stir in mayonnaise, yogurt, garlic, coriander, salt and pepper.

▪ **Halve** tomatoes crosswise and remove seeds; cut into small pieces. Add to pasta along with kidney beans and daikon. Spoon dressing over mixture and toss gently to combine. Taste and adjust seasoning if necessary.

*Makes 4 servings.*

**Wasabi:** Although this root, whose flavor is reminiscent of strong horseradish, is most often used as a condiment for sushi or sashimi, it is ideal for adding depth and excitement to creamy dishes, too.

Wasabi is usually sold as a dehydrated powder. Always taste wasabi paste before you add it to your cooking, since brands vary in strength. If you can't find wasabi in your local market, substitute grated fresh horseradish root to taste.

# POMEGRANATE COUS COUS IN PITAS

I've taken inspiration for this dish from Turkey, where pomegranate molasses is often used to add a fruity tartness to foods. You can stuff pitas with this concoction or eat it on its own as a side dish.

| | |
|---|---|
| 1 cup | instant cous cous |
| 1 1/4 cups | boiling vegetable stock |
| 1/2 cup | bottled pimento or roasted red pepper, drained |
| 1/4 cup | lightly packed fresh parsley leaves |
| 2 tbsp | lemon juice |
| 2 tbsp | pomegranate molasses |
| 1/2 tsp | each salt and pepper |
| 1/2 tsp | granulated sugar |
| 1/4 tsp | paprika |
| 1/3 cup | extra virgin olive oil |
| 2 | small tomatoes, seeded and chopped |
| 2 | green onions, thinly sliced |
| 1 cup | finely chopped English cucumber |
| 4 | pita breads |
| | Lettuce leaves |

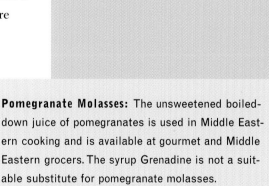

■ **Place** cous cous in large bowl. Pour in vegetable stock. Cover and let stand for 5 minutes. Fluff with a fork and let cool at least 10 minutes or until room temperature.

■ **Meanwhile**, in food processor or blender combine pimento, parsley, lemon juice, pomegranate molasses, salt, pepper, sugar and paprika. Process until smooth. With motor running, drizzle in olive oil.

■ **Stir** dressing, tomatoes, green onions and cucumber into cous cous until well combined. Taste and adjust seasoning if necessary.

■ **Cut** a strip off one side of each pita; separate halves to make a pocket in bread. Line with lettuce and divide cous cous mixture evenly between breads.

*Makes 4 sandwiches.*

**Pomegranate Molasses:** The unsweetened boiled-down juice of pomegranates is used in Middle Eastern cooking and is available at gourmet and Middle Eastern grocers. The syrup Grenadine is not a suitable substitute for pomegranate molasses.

# ORZO GORENG

Nasi goreng is an Indonesian dish that my in-laws love. This modified version uses orzo, which cooks quickly but still gives me a similar finished product. The dish itself is quite mild, so if you're like my father-in-law, you'll want to add lots of spicy sambal oelek at the table!

| | |
|---|---|
| 1 | **carrot**, chopped |
| 1 1/2 cups | **orzo** |
| 2 | eggs |
| 1 tsp | red pepper flakes |
| 1/4 tsp | salt |
| 1/3 cup | vegetable oil |
| 1 | large onion, finely chopped |
| 1 tsp | **shrimp paste** or minced prawns in spice (see page 99) |
| 3 | cloves garlic, minced |
| 1 cup | finely chopped **cucumber** |
| 2 tbsp | ketjap manis |
| 1 tbsp | lime juice |
| 1/2 cup | thinly sliced **green onions** |
| | Sambal oelek |

■ **In large** pot of boiling salted water, cook carrots for 5 minutes or until almost tender; remove with a slotted spoon and reserve. Add orzo and cook for 4 minutes or until almost al dente; drain well and reserve.

■ **Using** a fork, beat together eggs, red pepper flakes and salt. Heat 1 tbsp of the oil in nonstick skillet set over medium heat. Pour egg mixture into pan and cook for 2 minutes; cover and cook for 2 more minutes or until lightly browned on the bottom and set on top. Run a knife around the edge of the pan and roll into a cylinder. Transfer to a plate and cut into thin strips.

■ **Heat** 2 tbsp of the oil in wok or deep skillet set over medium heat. Add onion and shrimp paste and cook, stirring often and breaking up shrimp paste, for 5 minutes; increase heat to high and stir-fry for 2 minutes or until onion is well browned.

■ **Add** remaining oil; stir in garlic, cucumber and carrot and stir-fry for 2 minutes. Stir in orzo and toss to combine. Sprinkle with ketjap manis and lime juice. Transfer to heated platter and sprinkle with green onions. Serve with sambal oelek on the side.

*Makes 4 to 6 servings.*

**Ketjap Manis:** This sweet, thick, treacle-flavored soy sauce is widely used in Indonesian and Malaysian cooking. If you can't find it at your market, you can use $1\frac{1}{2}$ tbsp dark soy sauce plus $\frac{1}{4}$ tsp molasses to achieve a similar flavor.

# Mango and Rice Noodle Salad in Lettuce Cups

**Exotic without being challenging, this combination of flavors is sure to be a crowd pleaser.**

| | |
|---|---|
| 2 oz | rice vermicelli |
| 2 tsp | rice vinegar |
| 2 tsp | lime juice |
| 1 tsp | liquid honey |
| 1/2 tsp | red pepper flakes |
| 1/2 tsp | finely grated lime zest |
| 1 tbsp | toasted sesame oil |
| 1/4 cup | vegetable oil |
| 1/4 cup | chopped fresh coriander |
| 1/2 tsp | each salt and pepper |
| 1 | mango, peeled and cut into julienne |
| 1/4 cup | very finely chopped red onion |
| 4 | Boston lettuce leaves |

■ **Place** noodles in large deep bowl; cover with boiling water and let stand for 2 minutes; drain well and reserve.

■ **Meanwhile**, in large bowl whisk together rice vinegar, lime juice, honey, red pepper flakes and lime zest. Whisking constantly, drizzle in sesame and vegetable oils until well combined. Stir in coriander, salt and pepper.

■ **Add** noodles, mango and onion; using two spoons, toss until well combined. Taste and adjust seasoning if necessary. Place equal amounts of mango mixture in each lettuce leaf.

*Makes 4 servings.*

**Mango:** Probably one of the best-tasting fruits on earth! Mangoes are native to India, the Far East and Southeast Asia and turn up in recipes from each of these regions. To choose an optimum mango, look for a firm, unwrinkled skin that yields slightly to a gentle touch.

# TAGLIATELLE WITH WASABI CREAM SAUCE

I know I've said it before in this book, but this is a really great noodle recipe! It's basically like an Alfredo sauce, but wasabi and ginger add a welcome new dimension that helps to cut the richness of the cream.

| | |
|---|---|
| 1/4 cup | pink pickled ginger |
| 12 oz | tagliatelle or fettuccine |
| 1 tbsp | wasabi powder |
| 1 1/4 cups | whipping cream |
| 1/4 cup | butter |
| 1 cup | freshly grated Parmesan cheese |
| 1/2 tsp | salt |
| pinch | pepper |
| | Chopped chives or green onions for garnish |

■ **Finely** chop half the pickled ginger; reserve. In large pot of boiling salted water, cook noodles for 8 to 10 minutes or until al dente; drain well and reserve.

■ **Meanwhile**, stir wasabi powder into 2 tbsp of the cream to make a paste. In large skillet, bring remaining cream and butter to a boil; reduce heat and whisk in wasabi paste, chopped ginger, Parmesan, salt and pepper. Add noodles and toss to combine. Spoon into heated pasta bowls and top with a tuft of pickled ginger and chopped chives.

*Makes 4 servings.*

**Pickled Ginger:** Also called gari or sushoga, this thinly sliced brine-cured ginger is served as a condiment with sushi. It is either pink or ivory and should be stored in brine in the refrigerator. Pickled ginger is unique in that it tastes both hot and coolly fresh at the same time. The brine is also useful as a flavoring agent. Available fresh at fish markets and Asian shops and in bottles at supermarkets.

# Noodles with Asian Roasted Red Pepper Sauce

The vibrant red of this delicious but spicy dish signals that it is hot stuff! Make your own roasted red peppers ahead of time or find them at upscale deli counters or in jars at the supermarket.

| | |
|---|---|
| 8 oz | medium rice stick noodles |
| pinch | salt |
| 3 | roasted red peppers, skins removed |
| 2 tbsp | vegetable oil |
| 1/4 cup | minced shallots or onion |
| 1 tsp | minced fresh coriander stalks |
| 1 tsp | sambal oelek |
| 2 | cloves garlic, minced |
| 1 tsp | chopped pickled ginger |
| 1/2 tsp | shrimp paste |
| 1 tbsp | mirin or medium sherry |
| 1 tsp | fish sauce |
| 1 tsp | aged balsamic vinegar |
| 1/3 cup | loosely packed basil leaves |
| 1 tbsp | lime juice |
| | Lime wedges for garnish |

■ **Place** noodles in deep bowl and sprinkle with salt. Pour boiling water over noodles and let stand for 5 minutes; drain well and reserve.

■ **Place** peppers in food processor and purée until smooth.

■ **Heat** oil in wok or deep skillet set over medium heat; add shallots and cook, stirring often, for 5 minutes.

■ **Add** coriander stalks, sambal oelek, garlic, ginger and shrimp paste; cook, stirring often, for 3 minutes or until garlic is softened. Stir in peppers, mirin, fish sauce and vinegar. Reduce heat and simmer for 3 minutes. Stir in basil and lime juice. Add noodles and, using two spoons, toss well to combine. Garnish with lime wedges.

*Makes 4 servings.*

**To Roast Peppers:** Cut peppers in half lengthwise and remove seeds and white membranes. Brush lightly with oil and place, cut side down, on a baking sheet. Roast in 375°F oven for 15 minutes or until softened. Increase temperature to 475°F and roast for 5 to 10 minutes more or until skins are blistered and dark brown. Let cool; slip off skins and discard. Keep peppers wrapped tightly in refrigerator for up to 2 days or in freezer for up to 1 month.

# SESAME NOODLES

This recipe is a good example of a "dry" noodle dish; that is, the noodles are tossed with just enough liquid ingredients to make them flavorful and moist but not enough to make them saucy. The effect is wonderfully delicious!

| | |
|---|---|
| 2 tbsp | sesame seeds |
| 2/3 cup | vegetable or chicken stock |
| 1/4 cup | tahini or smooth natural peanut butter |
| 2 tbsp | mirin or medium sherry |
| 1 1/2 tbsp | light soy sauce |
| 2 tsp | lime juice |
| 2 tsp | fish sauce |
| 1 tsp | granulated sugar |
| 1 tsp | sambal oelek or Tabasco sauce |
| 8 oz | pre-cooked chow mein noodles (about 1/2 pkg.), or 4 cups cooked spaghetti |
| 1/2 cup | cooked thinly sliced carrots |
| 2 | green onions, chopped |
| 2 tsp | coarsely chopped fresh coriander |
| | Lime wedges for garnish |

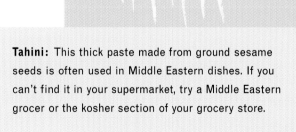

■ **In small** saucepan set over medium heat, constantly stir sesame seeds until golden and fragrant. Remove from pan and reserve.

■ **In same** saucepan set over medium-high heat, stir together stock, tahini, mirin, soy sauce, lime juice, fish sauce, sugar and sambal oelek. Bring to a boil and cook for 1 minute. Remove from heat and keep warm.

■ **In large** pot of boiling salted water, cook noodles for 1 minute or until heated through and almost tender. Add carrots and cook for 1 minute or until heated through. Drain well and toss with sauce. Sprinkle with green onions, coriander and sesame seeds. Serve with lime wedges on the side.

*Makes 4 servings.*

**Tahini:** This thick paste made from ground sesame seeds is often used in Middle Eastern dishes. If you can't find it in your supermarket, try a Middle Eastern grocer or the kosher section of your grocery store.

# Hot Mustard Sauce Chow Mein

**The interesting flavor combination in this one-dish meal will excite people who are bored with more familiar Asian flavors.**

| | |
|---|---|
| 1 tbsp | vegetable oil |
| 1 | small onion, sliced |
| 4 cups | chopped bok choy |
| 1/2 cup | sliced celery |
| 2 | cloves garlic, minced |
| 1 cup | chicken or vegetable stock |
| 2 tbsp | tamari or light soy sauce |
| 1 1/2 tbsp | dry mustard |
| 1 tbsp | white vinegar |
| 2 tsp | toasted sesame oil |
| 1 tsp | brown sugar |
| 1 tbsp | cornstarch |
| 12 oz | pre-cooked chow mein noodles, or 4 cups cooked fettuccine |
| 2 tbsp | chopped toasted peanuts or cashews (see page 76) |

■ **Heat** oil in wok or deep skillet set over medium heat; add onion and cook, stirring often, for 3 minutes or until slightly softened. Stir in bok choy, celery and garlic and cook, stirring often, for 5 minutes or until vegetables are lightly browned. Add stock, tamari, dry mustard, vinegar, 1 tsp of the sesame oil and brown sugar. Bring to a boil; reduce heat and simmer for 5 minutes or until celery is tender.

■ **Stir** cornstarch into 1 tbsp cold water. Make a well in vegetables and stir cornstarch into pan juices. Bring to a boil and cook, stirring, for 30 seconds or until thickened. Toss vegetables in sauce until glazed. Remove from heat and reserve.

■ **Meanwhile**, loosen noodles with your fingers; immerse in boiling salted water for 1 minute or until tender. Drain well and fluff with a fork; toss with remaining sesame oil. Place noodles on heated platter and spread vegetables over top. Sprinkle evenly with peanuts.

*Makes 4 servings.*

# STIR-FRIED JEWELS OVER CHOW MEIN

**One of the most appealing things about Asian cooking is that it is often as good to look at as it is to eat. In this stir-fry the vibrant greens and reds of the vegetables give this meal true eye appeal.**

| | |
|---|---|
| 12 oz | pre-cooked chow mein noodles, or 4 cups cooked spaghetti |
| 2 tsp | toasted sesame oil |
| 2 tbsp | each oyster sauce and fish sauce |
| 2 tbsp | mirin or medium sherry |
| 1 tbsp | granulated sugar |
| 1 tbsp | cornstarch |
| 1 tbsp | tamari or light soy sauce |
| 1/2 tsp | chili-ginger sauce |
| 3 | cloves garlic, minced |
| 2 tbsp | vegetable oil |
| 1 | each red and green pepper, sliced |
| 1 cup | halved snow peas |
| 1 | can (8 oz/227 g) sliced water chestnuts, drained |
| 2 tbsp | chopped toasted peanuts or almonds (see page 76) |

■ **Loosen** noodles with your fingers; immerse in boiling water for 1 minute. Drain well and toss with 1 tsp of the sesame oil. Reserve.

■ **Meanwhile**, whisk together oyster sauce, fish sauce, mirin, sugar, cornstarch, tamari, remaining sesame oil, chili-ginger sauce and garlic until well combined.

■ **Heat** vegetable oil in wok or deep heavy skillet set over high heat; add peppers and stir-fry for 3 to 4 minutes or until browned. Stir in snow peas and water chestnuts. Push vegetables up sides of pan to make a well. Stir cornstarch mixture and pour into well. Cook, stirring, for 1 to 2 minutes or until thick and glossy. Stir vegetables into sauce.

■ **Place** noodles on heated platter; top with vegetables. Sprinkle evenly with peanuts.

*Makes 4 servings.*

# Red Curry–Coconut Stir-Fry

Thai red curry paste differs greatly from Indian curry, so be sure you've got the right product before you start cooking. In my area there are several brands of Thai red curry paste on the market; I've tried them all, and the differences between them are negligible.

| | |
|---|---|
| 12 oz | pre-cooked chow mein noodles |
| 1 tsp | toasted sesame oil |
| 2 tbsp | vegetable oil |
| 1 tbsp | Thai red curry paste |
| 1 | red pepper, chopped |
| 1 cup | chopped zucchini |
| 1 cup | unsweetened coconut milk |
| 2/3 cup | vegetable stock |
| 1/4 cup | fish sauce |
| 1 tbsp | brown sugar |
| 1/4 cup | chopped fresh basil |
| 2 tbsp | chopped fresh coriander |

■ **Loosen** noodles with your fingers; immerse in boiling salted water for 1 minute. Drain well and toss with sesame oil. Reserve.

■ **Heat** vegetable oil in wok or deep skillet set over high heat; add curry paste and cook, stirring, for 1 minute or until fragrant. Stir in red pepper and zucchini and stir-fry for 2 minutes. Stir in coconut milk, stock, fish sauce and brown sugar; bring to a boil and simmer for 5 minutes. Stir in basil, coriander and noodles; cook, tossing to combine, for 2 minutes or until well mixed and heated through.

*Makes 4 servings.*

**Chow Mein Noodles:** I'm a big fan of chow mein noodles because they have a nice chewy texture and hold up so well in a wok. Chow mein noodles contain eggs and have a slightly crinkled texture that makes them ideal for holding a sauce or supporting a stir-fry. Look for them in the refrigerator section at your grocer or in the Asian section where dried chow mein noodles can sometimes be found. If you're using dried noodles in a recipe that calls for pre-cooked noodles, follow the package instructions for cooking.

# SUPERLATIVE VEGETABLE CHOW MEIN

This is my take on a "classic" North American–style chow mein; in fact, the flavors in this chow mein are so mainstream that even my dad will eat it! You can use whatever quick-cooking veggies you have on hand.

| | |
|---|---|
| 12 oz | pre-cooked chow mein noodles |
| 1 tbsp | toasted sesame oil |
| 1 cup | vegetable or chicken stock |
| 1/2 cup | light soy sauce |
| 3 tbsp | oyster sauce and hoisin sauce |
| 3 tbsp | mirin or medium sherry |
| 1 1/2 tbsp | cornstarch |
| 2 tbsp | vegetable oil |
| 1 | clove garlic, sliced |
| 1 | each red and green pepper, cut into long, thin strips |
| 1 cup | chopped bok choy |
| 1 cup | sliced snow peas |
| 1 cup | bean sprouts |
| 1/2 cup | chopped bamboo shoots |
| 3 | green onions, sliced |

- **Using** your fingers, loosen noodles. Immerse noodles in boiling water for 1 minute. Drain well and toss with sesame oil. Reserve.

- **In small** bowl or measuring cup, whisk together stock, soy sauce, oyster sauce, hoisin sauce, mirin and cornstarch.

- **Heat** oil in wok or deep skillet set over high heat. Add garlic and cook, stirring, for 1 minute; remove garlic and discard. Stir in peppers and bok choy and cook, stirring, for 2 minutes. Stir in snow peas and stir-fry for 1 minute; add bean sprouts, bamboo shoots and green onions. Make a well in the center of mixture by pushing vegetables up sides of pan. Stir stock mixture and pour into well; cook, stirring, for 2 minutes or until sauce is thickened.

- **Add noodles** and cook, tossing to combine with vegetables, for 2 to 3 minutes or until heated through.

*Makes 4 to 6 servings.*

### Variation

**Egg Chow Mein:** Before cooking vegetables, heat wok over medium heat. Add 1 tsp of vegetable oil; when hot, pour in a well-beaten egg. Cook for $1\frac{1}{2}$ minutes or until bottom of egg is well set and golden. Turn egg over and cook for 45 seconds or until cooked through. Remove to plate and chop; reserve. Just before serving, gently stir egg into chow mein.

# BUCATINI WITH TAMARI-ALMOND SAUCE

Bucatini is one of my favorite long pastas and it's great in this dish because it has the body to hold its shape and not be weighted down by the ground almond mixture.

| | |
|---|---|
| 12 oz | **bucatini** or linguine |
| 2 tsp | toasted sesame oil |
| 3/4 cup | toasted whole unblanched **almonds** (see page 76) |
| 3 tsp | **tamari** |
| 1/4 cup | packed fresh parsley |
| 1/4 cup | extra virgin olive oil |
| 2 | cloves garlic, minced |
| 1/2 tsp | salt |
| 1/4 cup | shredded **basil** |
| 1 tbsp | chopped oil-packed **sun-dried tomatoes** |
| 1 tbsp | finely chopped pickled ginger |

■ **In large** pot of boiling salted water, cook noodles for 8 to 10 minutes or until al dente. Drain well; reserve.

■ **Meanwhile**, heat sesame oil in small skillet set over high heat; add almonds and stir to coat with oil. Add 1 tsp of the tamari and cook, stirring constantly, for 6 to 8 minutes or until almonds are glossy.

■ **Combine** remaining tamari, 1/2 cup of the glazed almonds, parsley, olive oil, garlic and salt in bowl of food processor; pulse until very finely chopped but not pasty.

■ **Toss** noodles with almond mixture, basil, sun-dried tomatoes, pickled ginger and remaining almonds.

*Makes 4 to 6 servings.*

**Sun-Dried Tomatoes:** These have to be one of the ingredients of the '90s. If you have dried unreconstituted tomatoes you can use them in this recipe but you must first steep them in boiling water for 5 minutes or until softened. Drain off water (don't throw it out; sun-dried tomato water fortifies vegetable stock nicely) and pat dry. Drizzle tomatoes with extra virgin olive oil and combine with a bay leaf and a halved clove of garlic. Cover and let stand overnight.

# DANA'S DAN DAN NOODLES

Also known as Beggar's or Peddler's Noodles, Dan Dan Noodles are Asian street food sold from makeshift carts and bicycles. The authentic version uses pickled Szechwan vegetables, but these are very hard to find. I've substituted Indian lime pickle, but if you can find it, kimchi pickle is even closer to the real thing.

| | |
|---|---|
| 12 oz | pre-cooked **chow mein noodles** |
| 2 tsp | toasted sesame oil |
| 1/3 cup | tamari |
| 1/4 cup | **tahini** or smooth natural peanut butter |
| 1 tbsp | balsamic vinegar |
| 2 tsp | brown sugar |
| 1 tsp | chili oil |
| 1 | clove garlic, minced |
| 2 tbsp | vegetable oil |
| 1 1/2 cups | coarsely shredded **Napa cabbage** |
| 1 cup | vegetable or chicken stock |
| 2 tbsp | finely chopped Indian **lime pickle** |
| 2 | green onions, chopped |
| 2 tbsp | chopped toasted peanuts (see page 76) |

▪ **Loosen** noodles with your fingers; immerse in boiling water for 1 minute. Drain well and fluff with a fork. Toss with sesame oil and reserve.

▪ **In small** bowl or measuring cup, combine tamari, tahini, vinegar, sugar, chili oil and garlic. Stir until well combined; pour over noodles and toss.

▪ **Heat** vegetable oil in wok or deep skillet set over medium-high heat; add cabbage and stir-fry for 2 minutes. Stir in vegetable stock and lime pickle and cook, covered, for 2 minutes. Add noodles and cook, tossing to combine, for 1 minute or until heated through. Transfer to shallow bowl; sprinkle with green onions and peanuts.

*Makes 4 to 6 servings.*

# Quick Skillet Macaroni and Cheese

I absolutely adore baked ultra-cheesy macaroni and cheese but I rarely have the forethought to make it. So I created this quick version so that I wouldn't have to depend on less than satisfying frozen or packaged versions.

| | |
|---|---|
| 8 oz | elbow macaroni |
| 2 tbsp | butter |
| 1 | onion, chopped |
| 1 tbsp | all-purpose flour |
| 3/4 cup | whipping cream |
| 3/4 tsp | pepper |
| 1/2 tsp | salt |
| 1/2 tsp | nutmeg |
| 1 | clove garlic, minced |
| 2 cups | shredded aged Cheddar cheese |
| 1 tbsp | chopped fresh parsley |

■ **In large** pot of boiling salted water, cook pasta for 8 to 10 minutes or until al dente. Drain well and reserve.

■ **Meanwhile**, melt butter in ovensafe deep skillet or shallow saucepan set over medium heat; add onion and cook, stirring often, for 7 minutes or until soft and golden. Add flour and cook, stirring, for 2 minutes or until flour is combined and mixture is light brown.

■ **Whisking** constantly, add cream a little at a time until well combined. Stir in pepper, salt, nutmeg and garlic. Bring mixture to a boil, stirring. Stirring constantly, add $1\frac{1}{2}$ cups of the cheese, a little at a time, until sauce is smooth and cheese has melted. Stir in pasta until thoroughly coated with sauce. Sprinkle with remaining cheese and parsley; place under broiler for 2 to 3 minutes or until cheese is brown and bubbly.

*Makes 4 servings.*

**Variations**
**Broccoli Macaroni and Cheese:** Cook pasta for 3 minutes; add 2 cups small broccoli florets and cook for 5 minutes longer. Continue as above.
**French Onion Macaroni and Cheese:** Increase onions to 2 and cook as directed; sprinkle with 1 tsp granulated sugar and cook for 1 minute longer or until well caramelized. Add 1 tbsp medium sherry and $\frac{1}{2}$ tsp Worcestershire sauce, stirring to scrape up any cooked-on bits. Continue as above, substituting Gruyère for Cheddar.

# Honey-Glazed Snap Peas and Noodles

Packed with flavor, color and fiber, this great-tasting dish is an excellent way to get your family to eat healthfully. Shanghai, udon and wonton noodles work equally well in this recipe.

| | |
|---|---|
| 1 | pkg. (400 g) pre-cooked yellow **miki noodles**, or 4 cups cooked bucatini |
| 2 tsp | vegetable oil |
| 1 | onion, thinly sliced |
| 1 tbsp | minced **gingerroot** |
| 2 | cloves garlic, minced |
| 2 | carrots, thinly sliced |
| 1 cup | vegetable or chicken stock |
| 2 tbsp | each **oyster sauce** and light soy sauce |
| 1 tbsp | rice vinegar |
| 1 tbsp | honey |
| 1/2 tsp | Tabasco sauce |
| 2 1/2 cups | trimmed **snap peas** |
| 2 tsp | cornstarch |

■ **Using** your fingers, loosen noodles and place in deep bowl. Cover with boiling water and let stand for 3 minutes. Drain well. Using a fork, separate noodles; reserve.

■ **In wok** or deep skillet, heat oil over high heat. Add onion and stir-fry for 2 minutes. Add ginger, garlic, carrots, stock, oyster sauce, soy sauce, vinegar, honey and Tabasco sauce. Bring to a boil; cook for 2 minutes. Add snap peas and cook for 4 minutes more.

■ **Dissolve** cornstarch in 1 tbsp cold water; stir into wok and cook for 1 minute or until thickened. Add noodles and cook, tossing, for 1 to 2 minutes or until heated through.

*Makes 4 servings.*

# EMBARRASSINGLY EASY ASIAN-STYLE PASTA PRIMAVERA

I like to recycle, and this is a great example of how I enjoy taking an old favorite and making it a new one. With just a few twists on the classic pasta primavera recipe we've got a funky, easy-to-cook new meal that is anything but humdrum.

| | |
|---|---|
| 12 oz | **radiatore**, fusilli or penne |
| 1 tbsp | olive oil |
| 1 | bag (16 oz/454 g) frozen Asian-style vegetables |
| 2 | cloves **garlic**, minced |
| 2 tbsp | tamari or light soy sauce |
| 2 cups | spaghetti sauce |
| 1/4 cup | finely chopped fresh **coriander** |
| 1 tbsp | finely chopped pickled ginger |
| | Freshly grated Parmesan cheese |

■ **In large** pot of boiling salted water, cook pasta for 8 to 10 minutes or until al dente. Drain well and reserve.

■ **Heat** oil in wok or deep skillet set over high heat; add frozen vegetables and stir-fry for 4 minutes or until hot. Add garlic, tamari and spaghetti sauce; bring to a boil and cook for 1 minute. Stir in coriander, pickled ginger and noodles. Cook, tossing to combine, for 1 minute or until heated through. Transfer to shallow bowls and serve with Parmesan cheese on the side.

*Makes 4 to 6 servings.*

# Snow Pea and Mushroom Stir-Fry in Black Bean Sauce

Black beans are best in sauces that have strong, assertive flavors, so here I've paired them with lots of garlic and other distinct flavoring agents to make a complex, satisfying dish.

| | |
|---|---|
| 1/4 cup | Chinese fermented **black beans**, rinsed |
| 2/3 cup | vegetable or chicken stock |
| 1/3 cup | hoisin sauce |
| 1/4 cup | light soy sauce |
| 2 tbsp | ketchup |
| 2 tbsp | toasted sesame oil |
| 2 tbsp | rice vinegar |
| 1 tbsp | liquid honey |
| 1 tbsp | **Dijon** mustard |
| 1 tbsp | vegetable oil |
| 1 | small onion, chopped |
| 2 cups | thinly sliced button **mushrooms** |
| 3 | cloves garlic, minced |
| 1 1/2 cups | halved **snow peas** |
| 12 oz | pre-cooked chow mein noodles |
| 1/4 cup | finely chopped toasted **cashews** (see page 76) |
| 1/4 cup | chopped **green onions** |
| 1 tbsp | lime juice |

■ **Place** beans in small bowl; mash with fork. Stir in stock, hoisin sauce, soy sauce, ketchup, sesame oil, vinegar, honey and mustard.

■ **Heat** vegetable oil in wok or large deep skillet set over medium-high heat; add onion and cook, stirring often, for 5 minutes or until softened and lightly browned. Increase heat to high and add mushrooms; stir-fry for 7 minutes or until well browned. Add garlic and snow peas and toss to combine. Push vegetables up sides of pan to make a well; pour black bean mixture into well and cook, stirring, for 1 minute or until thickened. Stir in vegetables until coated. Cover and remove from heat.

■ **Meanwhile**, gently loosen noodles with your fingers; immerse in large pot of boiling salted water for 1 minute. Drain well. Fluff with a fork and place in shallow bowl. Pour black bean mixture over top. Sprinkle with cashews, green onions and lime juice.

*Makes 4 to 6 servings.*

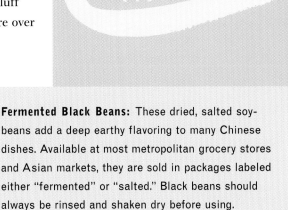

**Fermented Black Beans:** These dried, salted soybeans add a deep earthy flavoring to many Chinese dishes. Available at most metropolitan grocery stores and Asian markets, they are sold in packages labeled either "fermented" or "salted." Black beans should always be rinsed and shaken dry before using.

# Peas and Potatoes with Orecchiette

Orecchiette are small ear-shaped pasta from the Puglia region of Italy, where pasta is more often than not accompanied by vegetables. In this particular version from the region, the potatoes, peas and pasta combine to make a very nutritious vegetarian meal.

| | |
|---|---|
| 10 oz | orecchiette |
| 2 | large boiling potatoes (about 1 1/2 lb) |
| 1 cup | fresh or frozen tiny sweet peas |
| 3 tbsp | extra virgin olive oil |
| 1 | clove garlic, minced |
| 1/2 tsp | red pepper flakes |
| 1 cup | vegetable or chicken stock |
| 1/2 cup | freshly grated Asiago cheese |
| | Salt and pepper |

■ **In large** pot of boiling salted water, cook pasta for 7 minutes.

■ **Meanwhile**, peel potatoes and cut into 1/2-inch cubes. Add to pasta and cook for 3 minutes longer or until potatoes are tender and pasta is al dente; add peas and cook for 30 seconds or until peas are heated through. Drain well and reserve.

■ **Heat** oil in large deep skillet set over medium heat; add garlic and red pepper flakes and cook, stirring often, for 3 minutes or until garlic is translucent. Add stock and bring to a boil; boil for 1 minute or until slightly reduced.

■ **Stir** pasta mixture into stock; toss to combine and season with salt and pepper to taste. Serve at once with Asiago cheese on the side.

*Makes 4 servings.*

### Variation
In summer when greens are plentiful, substitute 2 cups firmly packed beet tops, arugula, spinach or Swiss chard leaves for peas.

# FAST AND FRESH FETTUCCINE

We don't often cook cucumber in North American cuisine, but it really is a nice way to enjoy it. If you eat fish, this pasta makes a great side dish to salmon or sea bass.

| | |
|---|---|
| 12 oz | fettuccine |
| 1 tbsp | butter |
| 3 tbsp | chopped capers |
| 2 tsp | dillseed |
| 2 cups | table cream |
| 2 cups | sliced seeded peeled cucumber |
| 1/4 cup | chopped fresh dill |
| 1/4 tsp | each salt and pepper |

■ **In large** pot of boiling salted water, cook noodles for 8 to 10 minutes or until al dente. Drain well and reserve.

■ **Meanwhile**, melt butter in large skillet set over medium-high heat. Add capers and dillseed; cook, stirring, for 1 minute. Stir in cream and bring to a boil; cook for 1 minute or until beginning to thicken. Stir in cucumber, dill, salt and pepper and cook, stirring, for 2 to 3 minutes or until cucumber is slightly softened. Taste and adjust seasoning if necessary. Add noodles and toss to combine; cook for 1 minute or until heated through.

*Makes 4 to 6 servings.*

**Capers:** Native to the Mediterranean, capers are the unopened flower buds of the caper bush. The buds are preserved in vinegar and salt or sometimes just salt alone. The very best capers are the tiny *nonpareils,* which come from Provence.

# Spinach with Capellini in Chili-Ginger Sauce

Pairing semolina noodles with Asian flavorings works well in this dish. The tender capellini becomes nicely coated by the sauce, resulting in a slurpily good meal.

| | |
|---|---|
| 1 1/2 cups | vegetable or chicken stock |
| 2 tbsp | chili-ginger sauce |
| 2 tbsp | hoisin sauce |
| 1 tbsp | light soy sauce |
| 1 tbsp | cornstarch |
| 8 oz | capellini |
| 1 tsp | toasted sesame oil |
| 1/2 tsp | ground Szechwan or black pepper |
| 1 tbsp | vegetable oil |
| 1/2 | red pepper, finely chopped |
| 1 | pkg. (9 oz/300 g) frozen chopped spinach thawed and well drained |
| 1 | clove garlic, minced |

▨ **In small** bowl, stir together stock, chili-ginger sauce, hoisin sauce, soy sauce and cornstarch.

▪ **In large** pot of boiling salted water, cook pasta for 2 to 3 minutes or until al dente. Drain well and toss with sesame oil and ground pepper; reserve.

▨ **Meanwhile**, heat vegetable oil in wok or deep skillet set over high heat. Add red pepper and stir-fry for 3 minutes or until browned. Stir in spinach and garlic until combined. Push vegetables up sides of pan to make a well; stir stock mixture and pour into well. Cook, stirring, for 1 minute or until thickened. Stir together with vegetables. Place noodles in a shallow bowl and spoon vegetable mixture over top.

*Makes 4 to 6 servings.*

**Szechwan Pepper:** Pepper is probably the most important of all spices. It's fundamental to cuisines the world over because it adds flavor of its own and helps to accentuate the flavors of other ingredients. Szechwan peppercorns are the dried red-brown berries of the prickly ash tree, which grows in China's Szechwan province. Also called brown or Chinese pepper, Szechwan pepper can have a slight numbing effect on your mouth, so use it sparingly.

# Asian Pesto and Noodles

The wonderful thing about cooking is that you get to travel the world without ever leaving your kitchen table. And, if you feel like visiting more than one country at once, all the better! By borrowing a little from Italy and a lot from Asia, this recipe lets you unite two cultures known for their way with noodles.

| | |
|---|---|
| 1/3 cup | each packed fresh coriander, mint and parsley leaves |
| 1/3 cup | chopped blanched almonds |
| 1/4 cup | freshly grated Parmesan cheese |
| 1 tsp | lemon juice |
| 2 | cloves garlic, minced |
| 1/2 | red chili, seeded and chopped, or 1/4 tsp red pepper flakes |
| 1/2 tsp | each salt and pepper |
| 1/3 cup | extra virgin olive oil |
| 12 oz | linguine |
| | Fresh coriander leaves for garnish |

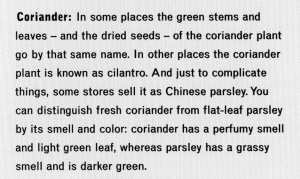

■ **In food** processor or blender, blend coriander, mint, parsley, almonds, Parmesan, lemon juice, garlic, chili, salt and pepper. With motor running, drizzle in olive oil and mix until smooth.

■ **Meanwhile**, in large pot of boiling salted water, cook pasta for 8 to 10 minutes or until al dente; drain well and return to pot. Stir in pesto; taste and adjust seasoning if necessary. Transfer to shallow serving dish and garnish with coriander leaves.

*Makes 4 servings.*

**Coriander:** In some places the green stems and leaves – and the dried seeds – of the coriander plant go by that same name. In other places the coriander plant is known as cilantro. And just to complicate things, some stores sell it as Chinese parsley. You can distinguish fresh coriander from flat-leaf parsley by its smell and color: coriander has a perfumy smell and light green leaf, whereas parsley has a grassy smell and is darker green.

# Spice Tent Orzo

Redolent of cinnamon and orange, this yummy side dish goes well alongside mildly curried potatoes, cauliflower and carrots.

| | |
|---|---|
| 2 tbsp | butter |
| 1 tsp | **cinnamon** |
| 1 cup | **orzo** or other tiny pasta |
| 1 1/2 cups | vegetable stock |
| 1/2 cup | orange juice |
| 3 tbsp | chopped dried **dates** |
| 1 tsp | finely grated orange zest |
| 1/4 tsp | each salt and pepper |
| 2 tbsp | chopped toasted **almonds** (see below) |

■ **Melt** butter in saucepan set over medium heat; add cinnamon and cook, stirring, for 1 minute. Stir in orzo, stock and orange juice. Bring to a boil; reduce heat to low and simmer gently for 6 minutes or until liquid is almost entirely absorbed.

■ **Stir** in dates, orange zest, salt and pepper. Cook for 1 to 2 minutes or until liquid is completely absorbed. Fluff with a fork; taste and adjust seasoning if necessary. Sprinkle with almonds.

*Makes 4 servings.*

**To Toast Nuts:** Spread nuts evenly on rimmed baking sheet and bake, shaking occasionally, in 350°F oven for 8 to 10 minutes or until golden brown.

# SQUASH RAVIOLI MEUNIÈRE WITH PINE NUTS AND CAPERS

No one will believe that a sophisticated meal like this one was cooked in under 10 minutes! With time savings like this, you'll be eating faster than if you ordered in.

| | |
|---|---|
| 1 | pkg. (12 oz/375 g) fresh squash or other **vegetable ravioli** |
| 1/4 cup | unsalted butter |
| 2 | **cloves** garlic, halved |
| 1/4 cup | **pine nuts** |
| 2 tbsp | chopped capers |
| 1 tbsp | chopped fresh **thyme leaves** (or 1 tsp dried) |
| 1 tsp | lemon juice |
| 1/2 tsp | each salt and pepper |
| 2/3 cup | freshly grated Parmigiano-Reggiano |

■ **In large** pot of boiling salted water, cook ravioli for 3 minutes or until it floats to the surface. Drain well.

■ **Melt** butter in deep skillet set over medium heat; add garlic and cook, stirring, for 1 minute. Increase heat to medium-high; cook for 2 minutes or until garlic is browned and sizzling stops. Add nuts and capers and cook, stirring, for 1 to 2 minutes or until nuts are golden. Stir in thyme, lemon juice, salt and pepper. Add ravioli and gently toss to coat. Divide between four serving bowls and sprinkle with cheese.

*Makes 4 servings.*

**Parmigiano-Reggiano:** This is the grand-daddy of Parmesan cheeses. Robust in flavor, there is no substitute for this cheese from north-central Italy. Although it is expensive, there are times – such as in Squash Ravioli Meunière, Penne with Middle Eastern Eggplant Sauce and Buttermilk-Walnut Quick Gratin – when its flavor is of such paramount importance that I insist you use the real thing.

# BUTTERMILK-WALNUT QUICK GRATIN

If you like creamy textures but don't like to eat a lot of cream, then this dish is for you. This combination of ingredients makes this gratin extremely comforting, while the buttermilk helps to keep down the fat content.

| | |
|---|---|
| 2/3 cup | freshly grated Parmigiano-Reggiano |
| 2 tbsp | chopped fresh parsley |
| 12 oz | **fusilli** |
| 1 | 2-inch-thick slice French bread |
| 1/3 cup | milk |
| 2/3 cup | chopped toasted **walnuts** (see page 76) |
| 1 | clove garlic, chopped |
| 1 cup | buttermilk |
| 2 tbsp | extra virgin olive oil |
| 1/2 tsp | each salt and pepper |
| 2 tbsp | melted butter |

▪ **Stir** together cheese and parsley.

▪ **In large** pot of boiling salted water, cook pasta for 8 to 10 minutes or until al dente. Drain well. Reserve in large bowl.

▪ **Meanwhile**, soak bread in milk for 30 seconds or until saturated; gently squeeze out excess milk and place bread in food processor. Add walnuts and garlic and pulse until almost smooth. Add buttermilk, oil, salt and pepper. Pulse just until combined.

▪ **Transfer** to small saucepan and cook over medium heat, stirring, just until warm. Stir into pasta and transfer to buttered baking dish. Sprinkle cheese mixture evenly over noodles. Drizzle with melted butter. Place under broiler for 2 to 3 minutes or until well browned. Serve immediately.

*Makes 4 to 6 servings.*

**Buttermilk:** In the old days buttermilk was the thin liquid left over after cream had been churned to make butter. What we buy labeled as buttermilk in stores today, however, is actually a cultured milk. This means that the milk has been pasteurized and fermented by a culture so that it has the acidic quality of real buttermilk that lends it its distinctive taste and makes it a good leavening ingredient.

# FETTUCCINE SULTANA

I like to think of this recipe as a base for a good meal. As the variations below illustrate, you can add lots of things to these noodles or you can use it as a side dish or as a bed to prop up grilled zucchini strips, cobs of corn or steamed mixed vegetables.

| | |
|---|---|
| 12 oz | fettuccine |
| large pinch | saffron threads |
| 1 1/4 cups | hot whipping cream |
| 1 tbsp | butter |
| 1/2 | small onion, finely chopped |
| 1 | clove garlic, minced |
| 1/4 cup | Riesling wine |
| 1/4 cup | vegetable or chicken stock |
| 1/2 tsp | each salt and pepper |
| 1/4 tsp | each grated lemon and lime zest |
| | Freshly grated Parmesan cheese |

RUBBING SAFFRON
BETWEEN FINGERS

■ **In large** pot of boiling salted water, cook pasta for 8 to 10 minutes or until al dente. Drain well and reserve.

■ **Meanwhile**, rub saffron between fingers and sprinkle onto hot cream; stir and let stand for 5 minutes.

■ **Meanwhile**, melt butter in large deep skillet or wok set over medium heat. Add onion and cook, stirring often, for 3 minutes or until softened but not browned. Stir in garlic and cook for 1 minute. Increase heat to high and add wine and stock; cook for 1 minute or until liquid is reduced to a couple of tablespoons. Stir in salt, pepper, lemon zest, lime zest and cream mixture. Bring to a boil; reduce heat to medium and simmer for 2 to 3 minutes or until slightly thickened. Add noodles and toss to combine. Serve immediately with cheese on the side.

*Makes 4 servings.*

**Variations**

**Tomato Saffron Sauce:** Add 1 cup chopped seeded peeled tomatoes when you add the cream.

**Asparagus Saffron Sauce:** Add 1 cup cooked asparagus tips when you add the noodles.

**Saffron:** It's no wonder saffron is the world's most expensive spice: to make a pound of it you need to hand pick the stamens from more than a quarter million crocus flowers. To preserve its potency, purchase saffron in small amounts and store in airtight containers in a cool, dark place.

# SPINACH NOODLES WITH SPICY GREEN CURRY

The Japanese spinach noodles available at my local grocery store are the most beautiful delicate green I've ever seen. (I love the color so much I matched a noodle to a paint chip and painted a room in my house this restful shade of green.)

If you can't get the fast-cooking Japanese noodles I call for, you can use another spinach pasta, although the incredible color of this dish will be compromised.

| | |
|---|---|
| 12 oz | dried Japanese spinach noodles or spinach spaghetti |
| 1/4 cup | vegetable oil |
| 3 tbsp | Thai green curry paste |
| 1 tbsp | fish sauce |
| 1/2 tsp | granulated sugar |
| 2 cups | French or regular green beans, halved lengthwise |
| 1/2 cup | unsweetened coconut milk |
| 1/2 cup | vegetable stock |
| 1/4 cup | finely chopped fresh basil |
| 2 tbsp | finely chopped fresh coriander |
| 1 tbsp | lime juice |
| | Lime wedges for garnish |

■ **In large** pot of boiling salted water, cook noodles for 5 minutes or until al dente. Drain well and reserve.

■ **Meanwhile**, heat oil in wok set over high heat. Add curry paste and cook, stirring, for 1 minute or until fragrant. Stir in fish sauce and sugar. Add green beans and stir-fry for 3 minutes. Stir in coconut milk and stock and bring to a boil; cook for 3 minutes or until beans are tender. Stir in basil, coriander and lime juice; add noodles and cook, tossing to combine, for 1 minute or until heated through. Serve with lime wedges on the side.

*Makes 4 servings.*

# SPAGHETTI WITH MINTED PEA SAUCE

This dish is so evocative of springtime – fresh, vivid green, and great tasting too. My mother loves it; in fact, she gets visibly excited when she hears it's going to be made. If only everything I made for my family had the same effect!

| | |
|---|---|
| 12 oz | spaghetti |
| 1 tbsp | salt |
| 4 cups | fresh or thawed frozen peas |
| 3 tbsp | chopped fresh mint |
| | (or 1 1/2 tsp dried) |
| 1/4 tsp | granulated sugar |
| 1/4 tsp | pepper |
| 3/4 cup | hot whipping cream |
| 1/4 cup | sour cream |
| | Fresh mint sprigs for garnish |

▪ **In large** pot of boiling salted water, cook noodles for 8 to 10 minutes or until al dente. Drain well. Reserve in large bowl.

▪ **Meanwhile**, in saucepan of boiling water, dissolve all but 1/4 tsp of the salt. Add peas and blanch for 2 minutes. Drain and rinse under cold water until cool; drain well.

▪ **Place** peas, mint, sugar, remaining salt and pepper in blender or food processor; purée until very smooth. Pour in cream and sour cream and blend well. Toss with noodles; garnish with sprigs of mint.

*Makes 4 servings.*

**Tip:** Although the amount of salt in this recipe may sound excessive, it's needed to control the pH balance of the peas so that they remain bright green and don't become muddy looking as they cook.

# 3°
# MINUTES

# Asian Pear Salad with Cranberry Dressing

Another uncommon but delicious combination, this recipe is packed with crunch and flavor. The dressing can be made ahead so that the salad is thrown together in mere minutes.

| | |
|---|---|
| 6 oz | farfalle or other short pasta |
| 1 cup | cranberry cocktail |
| 2 tbsp | tamari |
| 1 tbsp | minced onion |
| 1 tsp | Dijon mustard |
| 2 | cloves garlic, minced |
| $1/2$ tsp | each salt and pepper |
| $1/3$ cup | extra virgin olive oil |
| 1 | Asian pear or slightly underripe Bartlett pear, cored and finely chopped |
| 4 | green onions, chopped |
| $1/3$ cup | finely chopped celery |
| $1/3$ cup | toasted pecan halves (see page 76) |
| $1/3$ cup | dried cranberries |

■ **In large** pot of boiling salted water, cook pasta for 8 to 10 minutes or until al dente. Drain; cool under cold running water and drain well. Reserve.

■ **Combine** cranberry cocktail and tamari in small saucepan set over high heat; bring to a boil and cook for 8 minutes or until reduced to a syrupy glaze. Cool slightly; stir in onion, mustard, garlic, salt and pepper. Whisking constantly, drizzle in olive oil until well combined.

■ **In large** bowl, combine noodles, pear, green onions and celery. Drizzle with dressing and toss to combine. Just before serving, stir in pecans and cranberries.

*Makes 4 to 6 servings.*

**Asian Pears:** Sort of a cross between a pear and an apple, Asian pears have a crisp grainy texture and a great apple flavor. They look like an oversized speckled russet apple and should be handled gingerly, since they bruise quite easily. If you have a choice, buy imported Asian pears. They seem to have more flavor than the domestic I've tried.

# FIERY COCONUT NOODLE SOUP

This soup is great as a starter course for an Asian-themed dinner party because it's light textured and full of palate-bracing flavor.

| | |
|---|---|
| 6 oz | pre-cooked soba noodles (1/2 pkg.), or 2 cups cooked whole wheat spaghetti |
| 1 tsp | toasted sesame oil |
| 3 cups | unsweetened coconut milk |
| 2 1/2 cups | vegetable stock |
| 2 tbsp | fish sauce |
| 2 tbsp | grated gingerroot |
| 2 tbsp | lime juice |
| 1 tbsp | mild curry paste |
| 2 tsp | grated lime zest |
| 2 | stalks lemongrass, tender inner leaves only, cut into 1-inch lengths |
| 1 | large red chili, seeded and finely chopped, or 1 tsp sambal oelek |
| 1/2 | red pepper, finely diced |
| 1/4 cup | 1-inch chive pieces |
| | Fresh coriander sprigs for garnish |

■ **Loosen** noodles with your fingers. Place in colander and pour boiling water over top; drain well. Fluff noodles with a fork. Toss with sesame oil and reserve.

■ **In large** saucepan set over high heat, combine coconut milk, stock, fish sauce, ginger, lime juice, curry paste, lime zest, lemongrass and chili; bring to a boil. Reduce heat and simmer for 15 minutes. Strain and discard solids. Return liquid to saucepan and bring to a boil. Add red pepper and cook for 3 minutes or until tender. Stir in noodles and chives and bring to a boil. Serve garnished with coriander.

*Makes 4 servings.*

**Soy Sauce:** Soy sauce is made by combining roasted soybeans, wheat, yeast, brine and a bacteria culture. The mixture is then aged for up to two years before being strained and bottled.

Soy sauce comes in dark and light varieties, the light sauce being aged for a shorter time than the dark. I prefer the flavor of light soy sauce; however, if you have only dark on hand it too will work well in my recipes as long as you use a light touch.

# Aromatic Leek, Soba and Shiitake Soup

This fragrant soup tastes rich and unctuous even though it contains no meat. Because of its subtle flavor, serve it as a starter, before any spicier dishes you plan to serve.

| | |
|---|---|
| 6 oz | pre-cooked soba noodles ($^1/_2$ pkg.), or 2 cups cooked whole wheat spaghetti |
| 1 tbsp | vegetable oil |
| 1 tsp | butter |
| 2 cups | sliced shiitake mushroom caps |
| 1 | leek, white part only |
| 2 | cloves garlic, minced |
| $^1/_4$ tsp | minced gingerroot |
| 4 cups | vegetable or chicken stock |
| 1 tsp | soy sauce |
| 1 | whole star anise (optional) |
| | Salt and pepper |
| | Chopped fresh parsley for garnish |

■ **Loosen** noodles with your fingers. Place in colander and pour boiling water over top; drain well. Fluff noodles with a fork and reserve.

■ **Heat** 2 tsp of the oil with butter in large saucepan set over medium-high heat. Add mushrooms and cook, stirring occasionally, for 5 minutes or until golden brown. Remove from pan and reserve.

■ **Meanwhile**, cut leek in half lengthwise; wash well and slice crosswise very thinly. Set saucepan over medium heat and add remaining oil. Stir in leeks, garlic and ginger. Cook, stirring often, for 7 minutes or until leek is very soft but not browned.

■ **Stir in** stock, soy sauce and star anise and bring to a boil. Stir in noodles, salt and pepper and cook for 2 minutes; add mushrooms. Taste and adjust seasoning if necessary. Garnish with parsley.

*Makes 4 servings.*

**Star Anise:** Also known as Chinese anise or badian anise, this spice, the star-shaped fruit of a small evergreen tree native to China, is an essential ingredient in Chinese five-spice powder and is much used in Chinese and Vietnamese cooking. There is no substitute for the exotic, deep, spicy, sweet flavor it imparts.

# Ruby-Stained Fusilli with Lemon and Dill

Both beautiful to behold and delicious to taste, this dish makes an excellent centerpiece to a buffet or multi-course vegetarian meal.

| | |
|---|---|
| 12 oz | fusilli |
| 2 tbsp | vegetable or olive oil |
| 1/4 cup | finely chopped onion |
| 1 | clove garlic, minced |
| 1 cup | puréed cooked **beets** (about 4 small) |
| 1 cup | vegetable **stock** |
| 1 1/2 tsp | lemon juice |
| 1 tsp | finely grated **lemon** zest |
| 1 | medium beet, cooked and chopped |
| 1/2 tsp | each salt and pepper |
| 2 tbsp | each chopped fresh parsley and **dill** |
| 1/2 cup | crumbled **feta** cheese |

■ **In large** pot of boiling salted water, cook pasta for 8 to 1O minutes or until al dente. Drain well and reserve.

■ **Meanwhile**, heat oil in large saucepan set over medium heat; stir in onions and cook, covered and stirring occasionally, for 5 minutes or until softened.

■ **Stir in** garlic, puréed beets, stock, lemon juice and zest; bring to a boil and cook for 2 minutes or until sauce is thickened. Stir in chopped beet, salt and pepper. Add noodles, tossing to combine, and cook for 1 minute or until heated through. Stir in parsley and dill. Transfer to shallow serving bowl and sprinkle with cheese.

*Makes 4 to 6 servings.*

STIR

**Puréeing:** The smoothest, most velvety purées are made in a blender or food mill. A food processor or hand blender will produce an acceptable but slightly grainy sauce.

# TORONTO MEETS SINGAPORE NOODLES

Here's a recipe that truly reflects the mosaic of our modern world. Vietnamese noodles, Indian spices and a lot of my personal taste make this noodle dish a true mongrel's delight.

| | |
|---|---|
| 8 oz | Vietnamese rice stick noodles |
| 3 oz | firm tofu |
| 2 tbsp | vegetable oil |
| 1 tbsp | toasted sesame oil |
| 1 tsp | mild Indian curry paste |
| 2 | stalks celery, thinly sliced |
| 1 | onion, halved and sliced |
| 1 | carrot, thinly sliced |
| 1/2 | each red and green pepper, thinly sliced |
| 2 cups | coarsely shredded Napa cabbage |
| 1 | clove garlic, minced |
| 2 tsp | grated gingerroot |
| 1 tsp | red pepper flakes |
| 1/2 tsp | each ground coriander, cumin and turmeric |
| 1/4 cup | vegetable stock |
| 2 tbsp | tamari or light soy sauce |
| 1 tbsp | brown sugar |
| 1 cup | bean sprouts |
| 2 tbsp | chopped fresh coriander |
| 1/2 tsp | salt |
| 3 | green onions, cut in 1-inch lengths |
| | Chutney |

■ **In large** pot of boiling salted water, cook noodles for 5 minutes or until tender; drain well. Fluff with a fork and reserve.

■ **Meanwhile**, cut tofu into small cubes.

■ **Heat** vegetable oil and sesame oil in wok or large deep skillet set over high heat. Add curry paste and cook for 1 minute; add tofu and stir-fry for 2 minutes or until golden. Remove tofu and drain on paper towels.

■ **Reduce** heat to medium and add celery, onion and carrot; stir-fry for 3 minutes or until onion is softened and lightly browned. Add peppers, cabbage, garlic, ginger, red pepper flakes, ground coriander, cumin, turmeric and stock; increase heat to high and stir-fry for 3 to 4 minutes or until vegetables are softened.

■ **Stir in** tamari and sugar. Add noodles and sprouts; cook, tossing to combine, for 1 minute or until noodles are heated through. Remove from heat and add fresh coriander and salt; taste and adjust seasoning if necessary. Sprinkle with green onions. Serve with chutney on the side.

*Makes 4 to 6 servings.*

# Spicy Spaghetti and Vegetable Toss

If you want great Asian taste without having to forage for unusual ingredients, this recipe is for you. If you live in an urban area, everything in this recipe should be available at your neighborhood grocery store.

| | |
|---|---|
| 1 | can (14 oz/398 mL) baby corn, drained |
| 12 oz | spaghetti |
| 1 cup | vegetable or chicken stock |
| 2 tbsp | tomato paste |
| 2 tbsp | grated gingerroot |
| 1 tbsp | ground coriander |
| 1 tbsp | brown sugar |
| 1 tbsp | cornstarch |
| 1 tbsp | soy sauce |
| 1 tbsp | toasted sesame oil |
| 2 tsp | mustard seeds |
| 2 tsp | rice vinegar |
| 1 tsp | cayenne pepper |
| 1 tbsp | vegetable oil |
| 1 | small onion, cut into chunks |
| 2 cups | broccoli florets |
| 2 | cloves garlic, minced |
| 1 | yellow or orange pepper, thinly sliced |
| 2 tbsp | chopped fresh coriander |

■ **Halve** corn cobs lengthwise.

■ **In large** pot of boiling salted water, cook noodles for 8 to
10 minutes or until al dente; drain well and reserve.

■ **In bowl** or measuring cup, whisk 1/2 cup of the stock together
with tomato paste, ginger, ground coriander, sugar, cornstarch, soy
sauce, sesame oil, mustard seeds, vinegar and cayenne pepper.

■ **Heat** vegetable oil in wok or deep skillet set over medium heat;
add onion and cook, stirring occasionally, for 5 minutes. Increase
heat to high and add remaining stock, broccoli and garlic; bring to
a boil and cook for 5 minutes or until broccoli is bright green and
stock is almost evaporated. Stir in yellow pepper and corn; toss to
combine.

■ **Push** vegetables up sides of pan to create a well. Stir stock
mixture and pour into pan; cook, stirring, for 2 minutes or until
thickened. Stir vegetables into sauce; add noodles and cook, tossing
to combine, for 1 minute or until heated through. Serve sprinkled
with fresh coriander.

*Makes 4 to 6 servings.*

BOILING WATER

# Coconut Jade Stir-Fry

Mmm! The wonderful aroma of this stir-fry will transport you to Southeast Asia. Don't forget to garnish with lime wedges; the tangy juice helps to heighten all the exotic flavors.

| | |
|---|---|
| 2 tbsp | vegetable oil |
| 1 | onion, chopped |
| 3 | cloves garlic, chopped |
| 1 | red chili, seeded and finely chopped, or 1 tsp Tabasco sauce |
| 2 | stalks **lemongrass**, outer leaves removed, halved lengthwise |
| 1 tbsp | grated gingerroot |
| 2 tsp | ground coriander |
| 1 tsp | ground cumin |
| 1 tsp | finely chopped **pickled ginger** |
| 1 tsp | brown sugar |
| 1 tsp | **shrimp paste** |
| 1 | can (14 oz/398 mL) unsweetened **coconut milk** |
| 1 cup | chicken or vegetable **stock** |
| 1 tsp | **lime** juice |
| 1 tsp | each light soy sauce and fish sauce |
| 1 cup | chopped green beans |
| 2 cups | coarsely shredded **Napa** cabbage |
| 1 cup | chopped zucchini |
| 8 oz | medium **rice noodles** |
| 4 | green onions, chopped |
| | Lime wedges and fresh coriander leaves for garnish |

■ **Heat** oil in wok or large deep skillet set over medium heat; add onion and stir-fry for 5 minutes or until lightly browned. Add garlic, chili pepper, lemongrass, grated ginger, ground coriander, cumin and pickled ginger and cook, stirring, for 1 minute. Add sugar and shrimp paste; stir until well combined.

■ **Whisk** in coconut milk and bring to a boil. Boil for 10 minutes or until thickened. Add stock, lime juice, soy sauce and fish sauce. Boil for 5 minutes or until slightly reduced and beginning to thicken. Add green beans and simmer for 3 minutes. Stir in cabbage and zucchini and cook for 3 to 5 minutes or until vegetables are tender and sauce is thick enough to coat a spoon well. Discard lemongrass.

■ **Meanwhile**, place noodles in deep bowl and sprinkle with salt. Pour boiling water over noodles and let stand for 5 minutes. Drain well. Add noodles and green onions to hot sauce and toss to combine. Serve garnished with lime wedges and coriander leaves.

*Makes 4 to 6 servings.*

COCONUT MILK

**Shrimp paste** is a pungent dried seasoning made from dehydrated prawns. It is sold in cans, jars or cakes and can be kept at room temperature indefinitely if placed in a tightly covered container.

# Super Szechwan Tofu and Noodle Supper

Tofu can be intimidating but it doesn't have to be. Half the challenge in cooking tofu lies in buying the right type for the right job. (See page 111)

| | |
|---|---|
| 12 oz | pre-cooked chow mein noodles |
| 1/2 cup | vegetable or chicken stock |
| 1 tbsp | each light soy sauce and oyster sauce |
| 1 tsp | cider vinegar |
| 1 tsp | toasted sesame oil |
| 1/4 tsp | sambal oelek or Tabasco sauce |
| pinch | granulated sugar |
| 8 oz | regular tofu |
| 1 tsp | cornstarch |
| 1 tbsp | vegetable oil |
| 2 oz | small button mushrooms, halved |
| 4 oz | green beans, stem end removed |
| 1 tsp | grated gingerroot |
| 1 | clove garlic, minced |
| 1 tbsp | chopped toasted peanuts (see page 76) |

■ **Loosen** noodles with your fingers; immerse in large pot of boiling salted water for 1 minute. Drain well; fluff with a fork and reserve.

■ **In large** shallow dish, whisk together stock, soy sauce, oyster sauce, vinegar, sesame oil, sambal oelek and sugar. Cut tofu into 1/2-inch cubes and place in marinade, turning to coat; let stand for 15 minutes at room temperature or covered overnight in refrigerator. Drain, reserving marinade; whisk cornstarch into marinade.

■ **Heat** vegetable oil in wok or deep skillet set over high heat; add mushrooms and stir-fry for 2 minutes. Stir in green beans, ginger, garlic and 1/4 cup water and cook, stirring often, for 7 minutes or until water is evaporated and green beans are almost tender. Stir in tofu and stir-fry for 3 minutes.

■ **Stir** in noodles, tossing until well combined. Push tofu mixture up sides of pan to make a well. Stir marinade and pour into pan; cook, stirring, for 1 minute or until thickened. Stir noodle mixture back into sauce. Transfer to shallow bowl and sprinkle with peanuts.

*Makes 4 servings.*

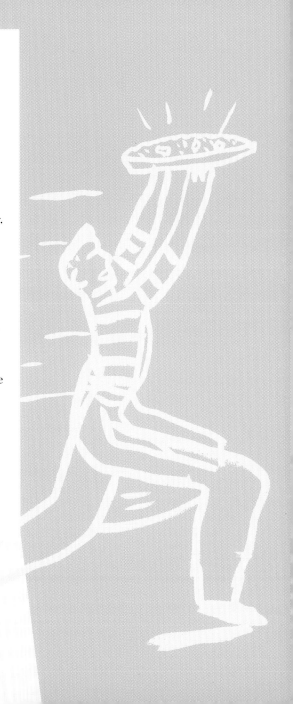

# Asparagus, Tarragon and Lemon Fettuccine

If you're craving the freshness of springtime, then look no further. Fresh asparagus, tarragon and lemon combine to make this a flavorful, delicate noodle dish.

| | |
|---|---|
| 1 tbsp | butter |
| 1 | small onion, chopped |
| 1 | small bay leaf |
| 1 cup | chicken or vegetable stock |
| 1/2 cup | dry white wine |
| 3/4 cup | whipping cream |
| 2 tbsp | chopped fresh tarragon (or 1 tsp dried) |
| 1 tsp | grated lemon zest |
| 1/2 tsp | each salt and white pepper |
| 12 oz | fettuccine |
| 8 oz | asparagus |
| | Freshly grated Parmesan cheese |

■ **Melt** butter in wide saucepan set over low heat. Stir in onion and cook, partly covered and stirring often, for 15 minutes or until onion is translucent and very soft. Stir in bay leaf, stock and wine; bring to a boil and cook for 5 minutes or until reduced to about $^{1}/_{2}$ cup. Strain through a fine sieve into a clean saucepan and discard solids.

■ **Stir** in cream and bring to a boil. Cook for 2 to 3 minutes or until beginning to thicken. Stir in tarragon, lemon zest, salt and pepper. Remove from heat and keep warm.

■ **Meanwhile**, in large pot of boiling salted water, cook noodles for 5 minutes. While noodles cook, cut asparagus into $1^{1}/_{2}$-inch lengths. Add asparagus to noodles and cook for 3 to 5 minutes more or until pasta is al dente and asparagus is tender. Drain well and return to pot. Pour sauce over top and stir to combine. Taste and adjust seasoning if necessary. Serve with Parmesan cheese on the side.

*Makes 4 servings.*

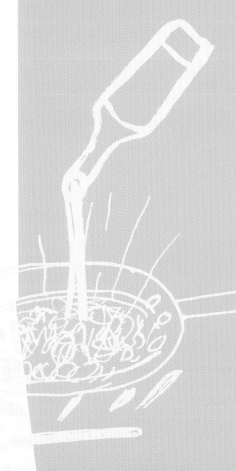

# Skoo-Bi-Do Rapini with Pine Nuts and Currants

Skoo-bi-do noodles, despite their ridiculous name, are one of my favorite pasta shapes. These little corkscrews get nicely tangled with the rapini so that each mouthful is full of flavor.

| | |
|---|---|
| 8 oz | rapini or broccoli (about 3 cups when chopped) |
| 8 oz | skoo-bi-do pasta or fusilli |
| 2 tbsp | olive oil |
| 1 | small Vidalia onion, or 1/4 Spanish onion, thinly sliced |
| 1/4 tsp | red pepper flakes |
| 1/4 tsp | each salt and pepper |
| 1/4 tsp | anchovy paste |
| 2 | cloves garlic, minced |
| 1/3 cup | stock |
| 1/4 cup | toasted pine nuts (see page 76) |
| 1/4 cup | currants |
| 1/4 cup | freshly grated Parmesan cheese |

■ **Cut** rapini into 3-inch lengths; wash and drain, leaving water still clinging to leaves.

■ **In large** pot of boiling salted water, cook pasta for 8 to 10 minutes or until al dente. Drain well and reserve.

■ **Meanwhile**, heat oil in large skillet set over medium heat. Add onion and cook, stirring often, for 8 minutes or until very soft. Add red pepper flakes, salt, pepper and anchovy paste. Increase heat to high and cook, stirring, for 1 minute or until onions are golden.

■ **Add** rapini and garlic and mix well; cook, stirring frequently, for 2 minutes. Add stock and cook, stirring often, for 3 to 5 minutes or until rapini is tender and pan juices are reduced to a couple of tablespoons.

■ **Stir** in pine nuts, currants, noodles and cheese. Transfer to shallow serving bowl.

*Makes 4 servings.*

**Rapini:** Also known as broccoli rabe, this vegetable is more closely related to the Brussels sprout than it is to broccoli. All three are members of the cabbage family, and both broccoli and Brussels sprouts can be used in basically the same way as rapini. Rapini is stronger tasting than broccoli and has a slightly bitter flavor that is an excellent foil to strong flavors like lemon, garlic and anchovy. If your rapini is mature (it's mature if the stalks are as thick as or thicker than pencils and it has developed buds shaped like broccoli florets), blanch in boiling salted water and refresh under cold running water before using.

# Vietnamese Rice Sticks with Vegetables and Peanut Sauce

It's hard to make a peanut sauce that doesn't become gluey and stodgy once it hits a noodle, but this one works well. Try to use Vietnamese rice sticks – they hold up well next to such a heavy sauce. If you do make substitutions, avoid udon, Shanghai and soba noodles, which get cemented together by peanut sauce.

| | |
|---|---|
| 1/2 cup | unsweetened **coconut milk** |
| 1/3 cup | smooth natural **peanut butter** |
| 1 tbsp | brown sugar |
| 1 tbsp | tamari or light soy sauce |
| 2 tsp | rice vinegar |
| 2 tsp | **lime** juice |
| 1/2 tsp | red pepper flakes |
| 1/2 tsp | each shrimp paste and **tamarind paste** |
| 2 | cloves garlic, minced |
| 1 | pkg. (8 oz/225 g) Vietnamese **rice stick noodles**, or 4 cups cooked spaghetti |
| 1 tbsp | vegetable oil |
| 1 | small onion, sliced |
| 1 | red or **yellow pepper**, sliced |
| 1 1/2 cups | coarsely chopped **bok choy** |
| 1 1/2 cups | small **broccoli** florets |
| 1/4 cup | vegetable or chicken stock |
| 1/4 cup | chopped toasted peanuts (see page 76) |
| 1 tbsp | chopped fresh coriander |
| | Lime wedges for garnish |

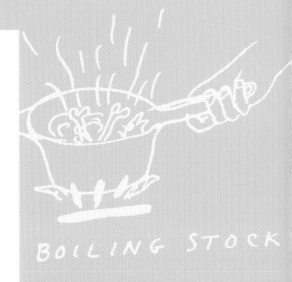

BOILING STOCK

■ **In blender** or food processor, combine coconut milk, peanut butter, sugar, tamari, vinegar, lime juice, red pepper flakes, shrimp paste, tamarind paste and half of the garlic; blend until smooth. Transfer to saucepan set over medium heat and bring to a boil; reduce heat to low and simmer for 5 minutes. Add about 4 tbsp boiling water, a tablespoon at a time, until sauce is thin enough to coat noodles. Remove from heat and keep warm.

■ **Meanwhile**, place noodles in large pot of boiling salted water for 2 minutes; drain well and fluff with a fork. Reserve.

■ **Heat** oil in deep skillet or wok set over medium-high heat; add onion and cook, stirring often, for 5 minutes or until browned. Stir in remaining garlic and red pepper and stir-fry for 3 minutes or until pepper is lightly browned. Remove pepper mixture and reserve.

■ **Add** bok choy, broccoli and stock; bring to a boil, cover and cook for 5 minutes or until vegetables are bright green and becoming tender. Return pepper mixture to pan; cover and cook for 3 to 5 minutes or until vegetables are tender. Add noodles and sauce and toss to combine. Transfer to shallow dish and sprinkle with peanuts and coriander. Garnish with lime wedges.

*Makes 4 servings.*

# Easy Cous Cous Salad with Sherry Vinaigrette

Dried blueberries transform this dish into a fresh approach to traditional cous cous salads. Even without the blueberries, though, this is a great warm-weather salad that goes really well with barbecued foods of all kinds.

| | |
|---|---|
| 2 cups | cous cous |
| 2 1/2 cups | boiling vegetable stock |
| 1 1/2 tbsp | sherry vinegar or red wine vinegar |
| 1 tsp | grated orange zest |
| 1 tsp | Dijon mustard |
| 1/2 tsp | granulated sugar |
| 1/2 tsp | each ground cumin, salt and pepper |
| 1 | clove garlic, minced |
| 1/3 cup | extra virgin olive oil |
| 1/3 cup | orange juice |
| 1/2 cup | each very finely chopped carrot, radish, celery and red onion |
| 1/4 cup | dried blueberries or currants |
| 1/4 cup | each chopped fresh mint and parsley |
| 2 | plum tomatoes, seeded and finely chopped |

■ **Place** cous cous in large bowl. Pour in boiling stock; cover and let stand for 5 minutes. Fluff with a fork and let cool for 10 minutes.

■ **Meanwhile**, in small bowl, stir together vinegar, orange zest, mustard, sugar, cumin, salt, pepper and garlic. Whisking constantly, drizzle in olive oil and orange juice until well combined.

■ **Stir** carrot, radish, celery, red onion, blueberries, mint and parsley into cous cous. Drizzle with dressing and stir gently, adding tomatoes, until well combined. Taste and adjust seasoning if necessary.

*Makes 6 to 8 servings.*

**Cous Cous:** A North African dietary staple, this tiny semolina pasta is made by rubbing dough over a sieve and then coating the dough granules in very fine wheat flour. Authentic cous cous requires steaming but the cous cous found in most grocery stores is pre-cooked and needs to be re-hydrated only.

# Stir-Fried Broccoli and Tofu with Rice Ribbons

Loaded with protein and calcium, this is the perfect quick dish for active people and their growing families.

| | |
|---|---|
| 2 tbsp | granulated sugar |
| 2 tbsp | each oyster sauce and fish sauce |
| 2 tbsp | mirin or medium sherry |
| 1 tbsp | cornstarch |
| 1 tbsp | tamari or light soy sauce |
| 1 tsp | toasted sesame oil |
| 1 | clove garlic, minced |
| 8 oz | regular tofu, cut into small cubes |
| 8 oz | wide rice ribbon noodles |
| 1 tbsp | vegetable oil |
| 1/2 tsp | red pepper flakes |
| 1 1/2 cups | broccoli florets |
| 1 cup | thinly sliced carrots |
| 1/2 cup | vegetable stock |

■ **In large** bowl, whisk together sugar, oyster sauce, fish sauce, mirin, cornstarch, tamari, sesame oil and garlic. Add tofu and toss to combine; let stand for 10 minutes.

■ **Place** noodles in large deep bowl; cover with boiling water and let stand for 5 to 6 minutes or until tender. Drain well and reserve.

■ **Meanwhile**, heat vegetable oil in wok or deep skillet set over high heat; add red pepper flakes and cook, stirring, for 1 minute or until fragrant. Stir in broccoli and carrots and toss to coat in oil. Stir in stock; bring to a boil, cover and cook for 5 minutes.

■ **Push** vegetables up side of pan to make a well. With a slotted spoon, remove tofu from marinade and add to wok. Stir marinade and pour into wok. Cook, stirring often, for 1 to 2 minutes or until sauce is thickened. Stir to combine well with vegetables. Add noodles and toss to combine.

*Makes 4 servings.*

**Tofu:** There's a lot to know about tofu, but you can be a successful tofu cook without earning a degree in soybeans if you learn to be a careful shopper. I've been specific in this book about what kind of tofu to use in each recipe. Buy the right one for each recipe and I promise you'll be happy with the results. A word of warning: regular, firm and extra firm silken tofu are not interchangeable with regular tofu with the same texture classifications. Silken tofu of any variety is too soft and custardy to hold up in stir-fries.

# Noodles with Fennel and Creamy Star Anise–Beet Sauce

A very unusual combination, if I do say so myself – but it's successful. If you eat fish or have carnivores to cook for, try these noodles with pan-seared sea scallops. Dee-lish!

| | |
|---|---|
| 1/2 cup | whipping cream |
| 3 | whole star anise, broken |
| 2 | cooked beets, chopped |
| 2 tbsp | orange juice |
| 1 tbsp | red wine vinegar |
| 1/4 tsp | each salt and pepper |
| 12 oz | pre-cooked udon noodles, or 4 cups cooked bucatini |
| 3/4 cup | warm chicken stock |
| 1 tsp | orange zest |
| 1 1/2 cups | cooked thinly sliced fennel |
| 1 cup | chopped beet or spinach leaves |
| 2 tbsp | chopped fennel tops |

■ **In small** saucepan set over medium-high heat, heat cream and star anise until steaming hot; remove from heat, cover and let steep for 5 minutes. Strain and discard star anise.

■ **In medium** saucepan set over medium-high heat, combine beets, orange juice, vinegar, salt and pepper. Bring to a boil; reduce heat, cover and simmer for 5 minutes. Uncover and boil for 4 minutes or until liquid is evaporated.

■ **Meanwhile**, loosen noodles with your fingers and place in large bowl. Pour boiling water over top and let stand for 4 to 5 minutes or until softened; drain well and reserve, keeping warm.

■ **Transfer** beets to blender and, with motor running, add stock, cream and orange zest until mixture is thin enough to lightly coat noodles. Taste and adjust seasoning if necessary. In a bowl, toss sauce with noodles, fennel and beet leaves. Sprinkle with fennel tops.

*Makes 4 servings.*

# PAN-ASIAN PENNE all'ARRABBIATA

The classical part of the name translates to "enraged penne," probably because it's so bored with staying at home in Italy! In this version penne takes flight to Asia, where it picks up some stimulating flavors.

| | |
|---|---|
| 12 oz | **penne** |
| 1 tbsp | sesame seeds |
| 2 tbsp | each chili oil and toasted sesame oil |
| 1 | can (28 oz/796 mL) crushed plum **tomatoes** |
| 2 tbsp | chili-ginger sauce |
| 1 tbsp | oyster sauce |
| 2 | cloves garlic, minced |
| 2 tbsp | chopped fresh **coriander** |

■ **In large** pot of boiling salted water, cook pasta for 8 to 10 minutes or until al dente. Drain well and reserve.

■ **Meanwhile**, in wok or deep skillet set over medium heat, constantly stir sesame seeds until golden and fragrant. Remove from pan and reserve.

■ **Heat** chili oil and sesame oil in wok set over high heat; add tomatoes, chili-ginger sauce, oyster sauce and garlic. Bring to a boil; reduce heat and simmer for 10 to 15 minutes or until thickened. Stir in coriander and pasta. Cook, tossing to combine, for 1 minute or until heated through.

■ **Transfer** to shallow bowls and sprinkle with sesame seeds.

*Makes 4 to 6 servings.*

**Oyster Sauce:** A Cantonese ingredient originally made from only oysters, salt and water, the sauce we buy today also contains caramel and cornstarch. But it still carries that savory, remarkably un-fishy flavor that lends so many Asian dishes depth and color.

# Firecracker Noodles

Some like it hot. Some like it hotter,
and this recipe is for them.

| | |
|---|---|
| 12 oz | pre-cooked chow mein noodles |
| 2/3 cup | vegetable or chicken stock |
| 2 tbsp | chili-ginger sauce |
| 2 tbsp | mirin or medium sherry |
| 1 1/2 tbsp | light soy sauce |
| 2 tsp | lime juice |
| 2 tsp | fish sauce |
| 1 tsp | granulated sugar |
| 1 tbsp | cornstarch |
| 2 tbsp | toasted sesame oil |
| 2 | red chilies, finely chopped, or 1 tsp sambal oelek |
| 1 | onion, thickly sliced |
| 2 | cloves garlic, minced |
| 1 | each cubanelle, sweet red and banana peppers, sliced |
| 2 tbsp | grated gingerroot |
| 1/2 tsp | red pepper flakes |

■ **Gently** loosen noodles with your fingers; immerse in large pot of boiling salted water for 1 minute. Drain well, fluff with a fork and reserve.

■ **In small** bowl or measuring cup, stir together stock, chili-ginger sauce, mirin, soy sauce, lime juice, fish sauce and sugar until well combined. Stir in cornstarch.

■ **Heat** oil in wok or large deep skillet set over medium-high heat. Add red chilies and stir-fry for 1 minute. Stir in onion and cook, stirring occasionally, for 5 minutes. Increase heat to high and stir in garlic, peppers, ginger and red pepper flakes; stir-fry for 5 minutes or until peppers are browned.

■ **Push** vegetables up sides of pan to make a well. Stir stock mixture and pour into well; cook, stirring, for 1 minute or until thickened and glossy. Stir vegetables into sauce. Add noodles and toss to combine; cook for 1 minute or until heated through.

*Makes 4 servings for spice lovers,*
*100 servings for the faint of heart.*

**Variation**
**Flame-thrower Noodles:** Increase red pepper flakes to 3/4 tsp and increase red chilies to 3; clear the dining room of flammable objects and go for it!

FIRE CRACKER

# PLAID NOODLES

Although tartan is generally evocative of Scotland, this dish is about as far away from haggis as you can get. Nonetheless, it's still pretty tasty and nice to look at, too.

| | |
|---|---|
| 8 oz | each beet or red Swiss chard leaves and stalks |
| 3/4 cup | vegetable or chicken stock |
| 2 tsp | cornstarch |
| 1/2 tsp | each Tabasco and Worcestershire sauce |
| 12 oz | linguine |
| 2 tbsp | olive oil |
| 1 | red onion, thinly sliced |
| 1 tsp | ground cumin |
| 2 | cloves garlic, minced |
| 1 tbsp | lemon juice |
| 1/4 tsp | each salt and pepper |
| 1 tbsp | extra virgin olive oil |

■ **Cut** beet greens into 1-inch-wide strips. Cut stalks into 1-inch-long pieces.

■ **In small** bowl or measuring cup, combine half of the stock, the cornstarch, Tabasco and Worcestershire sauce.

■ **In large** pot of boiling salted water, cook pasta for 8 to 10 minutes or until al dente. Drain well and reserve.

■ **Meanwhile**, in wok or deep skillet set over medium heat, heat olive oil; add onion and cook, stirring often, for 5 minutes or until softened. Add beet stalks, cumin, garlic and remaining stock; cook, stirring often, for 10 minutes.

■ **Increase** heat to high and add beet greens. Push vegetables up sides of pan to make a well. Stir stock mixture and pour into well; cook, stirring, for 1 minute or until thickened. Stir in lemon juice, salt and pepper. Toss vegetables in sauce to coat; taste and adjust seasoning if necessary.

■ **Add** noodles and toss to combine. Drizzle with extra virgin olive oil.

*Makes 4 to 6 servings.*

# SWEET AND SOUR PEPPERS AND FARFALLE STIR-FRY

Sautéed sweet peppers are always a tasty addition to a recipe, but when they're tarted up with a little sweet and sour they're simply divine. Make this colorful dish any time you want a genuine infusion of flavor.

| | |
|---|---|
| 2 tbsp | olive oil |
| 1 | onion, thinly sliced |
| 2 | cloves garlic, minced |
| 2 tbsp | chopped fresh oregano (or 2 tsp dried) |
| 1/2 tsp | each salt and pepper |
| 1 | each red, yellow and green pepper |
| 1 tbsp | red wine vinegar |
| 1 tsp | liquid honey |
| 1 tsp | tamari |
| 1 | can (19 oz/540 mL) stewed tomatoes |
| 1 tbsp | grated gingerroot |
| 4 cups | cooked farfalle (2 cups dried) |
| 1 tbsp | chopped fresh parsley |
| 1/4 cup | freshly grated Parmesan cheese |

■ **Heat** 1 tbsp of the oil in wok or deep skillet set over medium-high heat. Add onion and cook, partly covered and stirring often, for 5 minutes. Add garlic, oregano, salt and pepper; cook for 3 minutes or until onions are very soft. Increase heat to high and cook, stirring often, for 2 minutes or until onions are golden.

■ **Meanwhile**, cut peppers into long thin strips. Add remaining oil to pan and stir in peppers. Cook, stirring often, for 5 minutes or until peppers are brown around edges but still crunchy. Stir in vinegar, honey and tamari and stir-fry for 2 minutes or until peppers are well glazed.

■ **Make** a well in pan by pushing vegetables up the sides. Stir in tomatoes; bring to a boil and cook for 5 minutes or until thickened. Stir in ginger, pasta and parsley; cook for 2 minutes, stirring often, or until pasta is heated through. Remove from heat and stir in cheese. Taste and adjust seasoning if necessary.

*Makes 4 to 6 servings.*

vinegar

# CREAMY MEXICAN PASTA DINNER

A real winner with kids, this recipe is a cinch to put together – and it makes for some pretty tasty leftovers, too.

| | |
|---|---|
| 12 oz | skoo-bi-do noodles |
| 1 tbsp | butter |
| 1/4 cup | finely chopped onion |
| 1 | **red pepper**, chopped |
| 1 tbsp | chili powder |
| 1/2 tsp | ground cumin |
| 1 cup | chopped zucchini |
| 1 cup | vegetable or chicken stock |
| 2 | cloves garlic, minced |
| 1 1/4 cups | whipping cream |
| 1 cup | fresh or thawed frozen corn kernels |
| 1/2 tsp | salt |
| 1/4 cup | chopped fresh coriander |
| 1 tsp | lime juice |

■ **In large** pot of boiling salted water, cook noodles for 8 to 10 minutes or until al dente. Drain well and reserve.

■ **Meanwhile**, melt butter in large deep skillet or wok set over medium heat; add onion and red pepper and cook, stirring often, for 5 minutes. Increase heat to high; add chili powder, cumin and zucchini and cook, stirring, for 1 minute or until zucchini is lightly browned. Stir in stock and garlic. Bring to a boil; boil for 5 minutes or until reduced by about half. Stir in cream, corn and salt and boil for 2 minutes or until thickened. Stir in noodles, coriander and lime juice.

*Makes 4 to 6 servings.*

POURING CREAM

**Variation**
**Protein-Boost Mexican Pasta Dinner:** Add 1 cup cooked black beans with the corn.

**Chili Powder:** Besides ground dried chilies, commercial chili powders can contain garlic, onion, cumin, oregano, allspice and salt. Chili powder is not a substitute for the heat of dried chilies but it does add a nice base to Mexican-inspired dishes like chili con carne, fajitas and Creamy Mexican Pasta Dinner.

# Shanghai Noodles in Orange Sauce

Like udon noodles, Shanghai noodles have a heavier, pastier texture than most semolina or rice noodles. If you don't like a meaty noodle you may want to substitute an Italian noodle like spaghetti or linguine in this recipe.

| | |
|---|---|
| 1 | pkg. (10 oz/350 g) pre-cooked Shanghai noodles, or 4 cups cooked spaghetti |
| 1/2 cup | orange juice |
| 2 tbsp | mirin or medium sherry |
| 1 tbsp | tamari |
| 1 tbsp | toasted sesame oil |
| 1 tbsp | grated gingerroot |
| 1 tsp | brown sugar |
| 1/2 tsp | sambal oelek or Tabasco sauce |
| 1 tbsp | cornstarch |
| 1 tbsp | vegetable oil |
| 1 | onion, thinly sliced |
| 2 | cloves garlic, minced |
| 1/2 tsp | ground Szechwan pepper |
| 2 cups | small broccoli florets |
| 2 | carrots, sliced in coins |
| 1 cup | vegetable or chicken stock |
| 1 tsp | grated orange zest |
| 1 cup | sliced water chestnuts |
| 1/4 cup | chopped toasted cashews (see page 76) |

■ **Loosen** noodles with your fingers; immerse in boiling salted water for 2 minutes. Drain well, fluff with a fork and reserve.

■ **In small** bowl or measuring cup, combine orange juice, mirin, tamari, sesame oil, ginger, sugar and sambal oelek. Whisk in cornstarch.

■ **Heat** vegetable oil in wok or deep skillet set over medium heat; add onion and cook, stirring often, for 5 minutes or until softened. Add garlic and Szechwan pepper and cook for 2 minutes. Stir in broccoli and carrots. Add stock and orange zest and bring to a boil; cover and cook for 5 minutes. Stir in water chestnuts.

■ **Push** vegetables up sides of pan to make a well. Stir orange juice mixture and pour into well; cook, stirring, for 1 minute or until thickened. Add noodles and toss to combine; cook for 1 minute or until heated through. Sprinkle with nuts.

*Makes 4 servings.*

**Sambal Oelek** is a spicy relish style condiment used in Indonesian, Malaysian and Sri Lankan cooking. It's made from pounded chilies, salt, vinegar and tamarind.

# Pasta with Spring Onion Sauce

My one-year-old son adores this pasta dish, which may seem remarkable since it's packed with onions. But the long cooking time mellows the hot flavor onions naturally have and the result is a gentle onion taste that is surprisingly mild and fresh.

| | |
|---|---|
| 12 oz | **radiatore** or other short pasta |
| 3 tbsp | butter |
| 1 | small onion, very finely chopped |
| 3 cups | chopped **green onions** (about 3 large bunches) |
| 1/2 cup | dry **white wine** |
| 1/2 cup | chicken or vegetable stock |
| 1 1/4 cups | whipping **cream** |
| 1/2 tsp | each salt and white pepper |
| 1/4 tsp | freshly grated **nutmeg** |
| 1/3 cup | finely chopped fresh parsley |

▪ **In large** pot of boiling salted water, cook pasta for 8 to 10 minutes or until al dente. Drain well and reserve.

▪ **Meanwhile**, in deep skillet set over medium heat, melt butter; stir in onion and cook for 5 minutes or until softened. Stir in green onions and cook for 7 minutes or until very soft and just beginning to brown. Stir in white wine and cook, stirring to scrape up any cooked-on bits, for 2 minutes or until pan juices are reduced by about half. Stir in stock and cook for 5 minutes or until reduced to about 1/4 cup.

▪ **Transfer** to blender or food processor and blend until smooth. Return to pan and bring to a boil. Stir in cream, salt, pepper and nutmeg; bring just to a boil. Stir in parsley and noodles.

*Makes 4 servings.*

# PANGAEA CAPELLINI

At my husband Martin Kouprie's Toronto restaurant, Pangaea, one of his most popular dishes is angel hair pasta with jumbo Thai shrimp in a subtle tomato-ginger sauce. With this vegetarian version I recommend snow peas and baby corn for the garnish, but you can use any vegetables you like.

| | |
|---|---|
| 1 tbsp | olive oil |
| 1 | onion, chopped |
| 1/2 cup | dry white wine |
| 1 | can (28 oz/796 mL) chopped plum tomatoes |
| 2 | cloves garlic, minced |
| 3/4 tsp | jalapeño or Tabasco sauce |
| 1/2 tsp | (approx.) granulated sugar |
| 1/4 cup | chopped fresh basil |
| 1/4 cup | extra virgin olive oil |
| 2 tsp | grated gingerroot |
| 1/2 tsp | each salt and pepper |
| 12 oz | capellini |
| 2 cups | thinly sliced snow peas |
| 1 | can (14 oz/398 mL) baby corn, drained and halved lengthwise |
| | Freshly grated Parmesan cheese |

■ **Heat** 1 tbsp oil in large saucepan set over medium heat; add onion and cook for 5 minutes. Increase heat to medium-high and cook for 2 minutes or until onions are lightly browned. Stir in wine and cook, stirring to scrape up any cooked-on bits, for 1 minute or until reduced to about ¼ cup.

■ **Stir** in tomatoes, garlic and jalapeño sauce. Using the back of a spoon, crush tomatoes until pulpy. Bring to a boil; reduce heat and simmer for 10 minutes or until thick and saucy. Taste and, only if sauce is too acidic, add sugar. Stir in basil, extra virgin olive oil, ginger, salt and pepper; return to a boil. Taste and adjust seasoning if necessary. Remove from heat.

■ **Meanwhile**, in large pot of boiling salted water, cook noodles for 3 minutes; add snow peas and corn and cook for 2 minutes or until pasta is al dente and snow peas are bright green and tender. Drain well and toss with sauce. Serve with Parmesan cheese on the side.

*Makes 4 to 6 servings.*

# 20-Minute Vegetarian Pad Thai

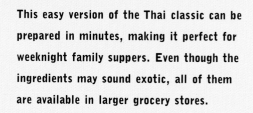

This easy version of the Thai classic can be prepared in minutes, making it perfect for weeknight family suppers. Even though the ingredients may sound exotic, all of them are available in larger grocery stores.

| | |
|---|---|
| 8 oz | medium rice noodles |
| 1/4 cup | vegetable oil |
| 1/2 tsp | sambal oelek or Tabasco sauce |
| 1 | pkg. (16 oz/454 g) regular tofu, cut into bite-sized pieces |
| 1 | red pepper, chopped |
| 3 | cloves garlic, minced |
| 3 tbsp | fish sauce |
| 3 tbsp | chili sauce |
| 2 tbsp | granulated sugar |
| 2 tbsp | minced prawns in spice |
| 2 tbsp | lime juice |
| 1 tsp | grated gingerroot |
| 1/3 cup | vegetable or chicken stock |
| 1 1/2 cups | bean sprouts |
| 3 | green onions, chopped |
| 1/3 cup | fresh coriander leaves |
| 1/3 cup | chopped toasted peanuts (see page 76) |
| | Lime wedges for garnish |

■ **Place** noodles in large bowl. Cover with boiling water and let stand for 5 minutes; drain and reserve.

■ **In large** wok or deep skillet, heat 2 tbsp of the oil and sambal oelek over high heat until very hot. Add tofu and stir-fry for 8 to 10 minutes or until well browned on all sides. Remove from pan and reserve. Add remaining oil and red pepper; stir-fry for 3 minutes or until peppers are becoming browned.

■ **Stir** in garlic, fish sauce, chili sauce, sugar, prawns, lime juice, ginger and stock; cook for 1 minute. Add noodles and tofu and cook, tossing to combine, for 1 minute.

■ **Add** bean sprouts and toss until mixed. Taste and adjust seasoning if necessary. Sprinkle with green onions, coriander and peanuts. Turn onto deep serving platter and serve garnished with lime wedges.

*Makes 4 servings.*

**Variation**

**Egg Pad Thai:** Omit tofu. After noodles are added to pan, make a well in the center of mixture and drizzle in 2 beaten eggs. Toss with noodles until egg is set. Proceed as above.

**Minced Prawns in Spice** is a sambal style mixture which contains prawns, peanuts, galangal, lemongrass and other spices.

# 45 MINUTES

# Malaysian Coconut Salad

This subtly flavored dish is a great introduction to the tastes of Southeast Asia, a region where the cooks seem to have a knack for making almost anything taste great. They cunningly combine sweet, salty and sour flavors to create some of the freshest, most surprising dishes on the planet.

| | |
|---|---|
| 8 oz | thin rice noodles, or 3 cups cooked spaghettini |
| 1 cup | thinly sliced cooked snow peas |
| 1/2 cup | bean sprouts |
| 3/4 cup | unsweetened coconut milk |
| 1 | stalk lemongrass, roughly chopped |
| 1/4 cup | chopped fresh coriander |
| 1 tsp | granulated sugar |
| 2 tbsp | finely chopped pickled ginger |
| 2 tbsp | lime juice |
| 1 tbsp | minced red chili, or 1 tsp Tabasco sauce |
| 1 tbsp | toasted sesame oil |
| 1/2 tsp | turmeric |
| 1 | clove garlic, minced |
| | Salt and pepper |
| 1/4 cup | finely diced red pepper |
| 2 tbsp | chopped toasted unsalted peanuts (see page 76) |
| | Lime wedges for garnish |

▪ **Place** noodles in large bowl. Pour in just enough boiling water to cover; let stand for 5 minutes. Drain well. Combine in serving bowl with snow peas and bean sprouts.

▪ **Meanwhile**, in small saucepan set over medium heat, combine coconut milk and lemongrass. Heat until steaming hot. Remove from heat, cover and let stand for 10 minutes. Strain coconut milk and discard lemongrass. Cool coconut milk until almost room temperature, about 15 minutes.

▪ **Whisk** together coconut milk, coriander, sugar, pickled ginger, lime juice, chili, sesame oil, turmeric and garlic. Drizzle over noodle mixture and toss to combine. Add salt and pepper to taste. Sprinkle with red pepper and peanuts and garnish with lime wedges.

*Makes 4 to 6 servings.*

# Broad Noodles with Mushroom Port Sauce

If you're looking for a fast, easy entertaining dish with roots in classical French cooking, then look no further. This earthy braise of mushrooms and leeks paired with a deep, rich sauce is the perfect recipe for any special occasion.

| | |
|---|---|
| 1 | **leek**, white part only |
| 1/4 cup | butter |
| 2 | cloves garlic, minced |
| 4 cups | sliced mixed **wild mushrooms** such as shiitake, portobello, morels and chanterelles |
| 1 tbsp | chopped fresh **thyme** |
| 1/2 tsp | each salt and pepper |
| 1/2 cup | finely chopped shallots or onions |
| 3/4 cup | port or **Madeira** |
| 1 | bay leaf |
| 1 | sprig fresh **rosemary** |
| 2 tbsp | all-purpose flour |
| 2 cups | dark vegetable stock |
| 12 oz | broad **egg noodles** |
| 2 tsp | truffle oil (optional) |
| 1 tbsp | finely chopped fresh parsley |

■ **Cut** leek in half lengthwise; wash well and slice thinly cross-wise.

■ **Melt** 1 tbsp of the butter in large cast iron or other heavy skillet set over medium heat; add leeks and cook, stirring often, for 7 minutes or until very soft but not brown. Stir in garlic and increase heat to high. Melt 1 tbsp of the butter and stir in mushrooms; cook, stirring often, for 8 minutes or until mushrooms are well browned. Stir in thyme, salt and pepper and cook for 1 minute longer. Remove from pan and reserve.

■ **Reduce** heat to medium and melt all but 1 tsp remaining butter. Stir in shallots and cook, stirring, for 3 minutes or until softened. Stir in port, bay leaf and rosemary; bring to a boil and cook for 5 minutes or until reduced and syrupy. Dust with flour and whisk to combine; cook, stirring, for 1 minute. Whisk in stock. Bring to a boil and cook for 7 to 10 minutes or until sauce lightly coats the back of a spoon. Strain sauce through a fine sieve and transfer to cleaned pan.

■ **Meanwhile**, in large pot of boiling salted water, cook noodles for 5 minutes or until al dente. Drain well and toss with remaining butter. Reserve in heated shallow bowl.

■ **Stir** mushrooms into sauce and reheat over medium heat until steaming hot; ladle sauce over noodles. Drizzle with truffle oil, if using. Sprinkle with parsley.

*Makes 4 servings.*

# Gnocchi with Rich Carrot Cardamom Sauce

Because the flavor of this dish is so intense and because it is so very rich, it is best suited to being one of many courses at a dinner party. An astringent salad of peppery greens is an ideal complement to this exotically flavored pasta.

| | |
|---|---|
| 3 cups | carrot juice |
| 1 1/2 tbsp | white wine vinegar |
| 1 | bay leaf |
| 2 tbsp | butter |
| 1/2 | small onion, finely chopped |
| 2 tbsp | all-purpose flour |
| 2 | cloves garlic, minced |
| 1/2 tsp | cardamom |
| 1/2 cup | mascarpone |
| 1/2 cup | freshly grated Parmesan cheese |
| 1/2 tsp | each salt and pepper |
| 1 lb | fresh gnocchi |
| 2 | green onions, thinly sliced |

■ **In large** saucepan, bring carrot juice, vinegar and bay leaf to a boil; reduce heat to medium-high and boil for 20 minutes or until reduced by about half. Discard bay leaf.

■ **Melt** butter in skillet or wok set over medium heat. Add onion and cook for 2 minutes. Stir in flour, garlic and cardamom and cook, stirring, for 1 minute. Whisk in carrot juice and cook, stirring, for 2 to 3 minutes or until thickened. Stir in mascarpone, Parmesan, salt and pepper. Remove from heat and keep warm.

■ **Meanwhile**, in large pot of boiling salted water, cook gnocchi for 1 to 2 minutes or until they float. Drain well and toss with sauce. Sprinkle with green onions.

*Makes 8 servings.*

**Cardamom:** Used since antiquity by the Egyptians, Greeks and Romans, cardamom is one of the world's most expensive spices. Fortunately, it is intensely flavored and a little goes a long way. Cardamom is a member of the ginger family but it has a deep aromatic, vaguely lemony taste all its own. It is sold as pods (which must be cracked to extract the seeds, which are the flavorful part of the plant), seeds or ground.

# Egg Noodles Marengo

By the time I was about twelve I was making dinner for my family almost every weeknight. One of the first times I varied from my mother's standard repertoire I made something called chicken Marengo, which, much to my family's surprise, was a hit! This vegetarian version borrows a lot from the French classic but excludes the ubiquitous chicken.

| | |
|---|---|
| 2 tbsp | butter |
| 2 cups | tiny button mushroom caps |
| 1 tbsp | vegetable oil |
| 1/4 cup | chopped onion |
| 2 tbsp | all-purpose flour |
| 1 cup | dry white wine |
| 1 1/2 cups | vegetable stock |
| 2 | cloves garlic, minced |
| 1 cup | peeled pearl onions |
| 2 cups | quartered and seeded cherry tomatoes |
| 2 tsp | finely chopped fresh thyme (or 1/2 tsp dried) |
| 1 tsp | each salt and pepper |
| 2 tbsp | chopped fresh parsley |
| 12 oz | broad egg noodles |

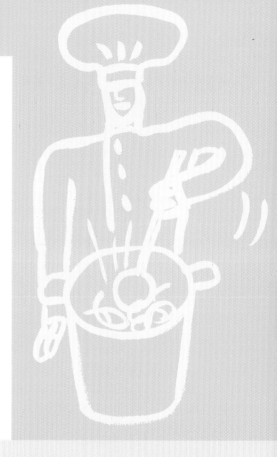

■ **Melt** butter in large heavy skillet set over high heat; add mushrooms and cook, stirring often, for 7 minutes or until browned. Remove from pan and reserve.

■ **Reduce** heat to medium and add oil to pan. Stir in onion and cook, stirring often, for 5 minutes. Sprinkle flour over onions and cook, stirring, for 1 minute. Whisk in wine and stock until well blended. Stir in garlic and pearl onions and bring to a boil; cover and reduce heat. Simmer for 10 minutes or until onions are easily pierced with a knife. Stir in tomatoes, mushrooms, thyme, salt and pepper. Cook for 5 minutes or until saucy and thickened. Stir in parsley.

■ **Meanwhile**, in large pot of boiling salted water, cook noodles for about 5 minutes. Drain well and place in shallow bowl. Ladle sauce over top.

*Makes 4 to 6 servings.*

**Tip:** To peel pearl onions easily, submerge in boiling water for 1 minute, then drain and rinse under cold water. Peel with a paring knife, working from the stem end to the pointed tip.

# PACIFIC RIM STOVE-TOP NOODLE QUICHE

Okay, so it isn't really a quiche, but it isn't really a frittata or a gratin either. Despite the nomenclature troubles, this recipe is a great reinvention of a typical pasta and tomato sauce dinner.

| | |
|---|---|
| 3 tbsp | vegetable oil |
| 1 | onion, chopped |
| 2 cups | sliced mushrooms |
| 1 cup | finely chopped zucchini |
| 3 | plum tomatoes, seeded and chopped |
| 2 | cloves garlic, minced |
| 2 tbsp | chili-ginger sauce |
| 1 tbsp | light soy sauce |
| 1/3 cup | chopped fresh coriander |
| 5 | eggs, beaten |
| 1/4 cup | whole milk |
| 1 tbsp | fish sauce |
| 2 cups | cooked spaghetti (4 oz dry) |
| 1 cup | shredded mozzarella cheese |
| | Fresh coriander sprigs for garnish |

■ **Heat** 2 tbsp of the oil in large skillet or wok set over medium heat; add onion and cook, stirring often, for 5 minutes. Increase heat to high and add mushrooms; cook, stirring occasionally, for 5 minutes or until vegetables are browned. Reduce heat to medium and stir in zucchini, tomatoes, garlic, chili-ginger sauce and soy sauce. Cook, stirring often, for 10 minutes or until tomatoes are cooked down and thickened. Stir in half of the coriander. Remove from heat.

■ **Meanwhile**, whisk together eggs, milk and fish sauce. Stir in noodles, mozzarella cheese and remaining coriander. In a nonstick skillet set over low heat; heat remaining oil. Pour egg mixture into pan; cover and cook for 5 minutes, shaking pan occasionally to prevent sticking. Continue to cook for 15 to 17 minutes or until egg is set and bottom of quiche is golden brown.

■ **Run** tip of knife around edge of pan to loosen quiche. Invert a large platter over skillet; invert pan and lift off. Slide quiche back into pan and cook for 3 to 5 minutes or until second side is lightly browned. Turn out onto platter; top with stir-fry and cut into wedges. Garnish with coriander sprigs.

*Makes 4 to 6 servings.*

**Make-Ahead Tip:** Stir-fry can be made up to 1 day ahead and reheated while quiche cooks.

**Fish Sauce:** This is the amber to dark topaz colored liquor that runs off when small fish are salted and then packed in wooden barrels to ferment for several months. It has a horribly pungent smell but adds an essential flavor component to many Thai and Vietnamese dishes. It keeps indefinitely without refrigeration.

# PENNE WITH MIDDLE EASTERN EGGPLANT SAUCE

I took inspiration for this pasta dish from the wonderful spicy eggplant served at Lebanese and Armenian restaurants. You could make this recipe spicier by increasing the cayenne, but I like it the way it is so I can taste the layers of flavors each ingredient adds.

| | |
|---|---|
| 1/4 cup | olive oil |
| 1 | onion, chopped |
| 2 | cloves **garlic**, minced |
| 1 tsp | ground cumin |
| 1/2 tsp | each ground coriander and paprika |
| 1/4 tsp | cayenne pepper |
| 1 | **eggplant**, peeled and cut into small cubes |
| 2 tbsp | lemon juice |
| 1 tsp | finely grated **lemon** zest |
| 1 tsp | salt |
| 1/2 tsp | pepper |
| 1 | can (28 oz/796 mL) tomatoes |
| 12 oz | **penne** or other short pasta |
| 1/4 cup | chopped fresh parsley |
| 2/3 cup | coarsely grated **Parmigiano-Reggiano or Asiago** cheese |

■ **Heat** 1 tbsp of the oil in large deep skillet or wok set over medium heat. Add onion and cook, stirring often, for 5 minutes. Stir in garlic, cumin, coriander, paprika and cayenne; cook, stirring, for 2 minutes or until fragrant. Increase heat to medium-high; add remaining oil and eggplant. Cook for 10 minutes, stirring occasionally, or until eggplant is browned. Stir in lemon juice, lemon zest, salt, pepper and tomatoes. Use the edge of a spoon to break up tomatoes. Bring mixture to a boil; reduce heat to medium-low and simmer, partly covered and stirring occasionally, for 20 minutes or until sauce is thick.

■ **Meanwhile**, in large pot of boiling salted water, cook pasta for 8 to 10 minutes or until al dente. Drain well. Stir noodles and parsley into sauce, tossing to combine, and cook for 1 minute or until heated through. Sprinkle with cheese.

*Makes 4 to 6 servings.*

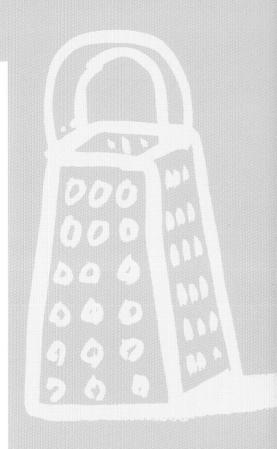

Parmesan cheese

# Caramelized Onion, Green Bean and Fusilli Toss

Caramelized onions are one of the most delicious things I can imagine. Unfortunately, they can't be rushed; if you try to brown the onions before they are soft and yielding, they'll scorch and taste bitter. So be patient. In this case it really is a virtuous quality!

| | |
|---|---|
| 2 | **Vidalia** or 1 Spanish onion |
| 2 tbsp | butter |
| 1 | clove garlic, minced |
| 1/4 tsp | each salt and pepper |
| 2 tbsp | granulated sugar |
| 1/4 cup | dry **sherry** |
| 1 tsp | Worcestershire sauce |
| 12 oz | **fusilli** |
| 4 oz | **green beans**, cut into 1-inch lengths |
| 2 tbsp | chopped fresh basil |
| 4 oz | Brie |
| 1/4 cup | chopped toasted **pistachio** nuts (see page 76) |

■ **Quarter** onions and slice thinly. Melt butter in cast iron or other heavy skillet set over medium heat. Add onions, garlic, salt and pepper; cook, stirring often, for 10 minutes or until onions are translucent. Increase heat to medium-high and cook, stirring often, for 4 minutes or until onions are just beginning to brown. Sprinkle with sugar and continue to cook, stirring often, for 6 to 8 minutes or until onions are very brown but not scorched. Add sherry and Worcestershire sauce and cook, stirring to scrape up any cooked-on bits, for 1 minute. Remove from heat.

■ **In large** pot of boiling salted water, cook noodles for 3 minutes. Add green beans and cook for 5 to 7 minutes or until pasta is al dente and beans are fork-tender. Drain well and add to onions.

■ **Set pan** over low heat and add basil and cheese; cook, tossing to combine, for 1 to 2 minutes or until cheese is melted. Taste and adjust seasoning if necessary. Sprinkle with nuts.

*Makes 4 servings.*

**Vidalia Onions:** Named for Vidalia, Georgia, where they are grown in abundance, a Vidalia onion is a small, very sweet onion that caramelizes well even without added sugar. Vidalia onions are available only during the winter and springtime. Spanish onions, on the other hand, are available year round but are not quite as sweet as Vidalias and are generally much bigger. Maui or Mayan onions are interchangeable with Vidalia onions. Due to their high moisture and sugar content, sweet onions do not store as well as cooking onions even when refrigerated.

# Thai Marinated Eggplant and Mushrooms with Rice Noodles

This is one of my favorite marinades, and I use it not only on eggplant but on zucchini, portobello mushrooms and flank steak, too. Don't be intimidated by the length of this ingredients list. These robust flavors combine easily to make a full-flavored meal!

| | |
|---|---|
| 3 tbsp | each **hoisin sauce** and fish sauce |
| 3 tbsp | lime juice |
| 2 tbsp | medium sherry |
| 1 1/2 tbsp | minced **gingerroot** |
| 1 tbsp | toasted sesame oil |
| 2 tsp | granulated sugar |
| 1 tsp | grated **lime zest** |
| 1 tsp | sambal oelek or Tabasco sauce |
| 3 | cloves garlic, minced |
| 2 cups | halved button mushrooms |
| 1 | small **eggplant**, peeled and diced |
| 8 oz | thin rice noodles, or 3 cups cooked angel hair pasta |
| 3/4 cup | vegetable or chicken stock |
| 1 tbsp | cornstarch |
| 3 tbsp | vegetable oil |
| 1 | green pepper, chopped |
| 1/4 cup | chopped toasted **cashews** or almonds (see page 76) |
| 2 | green onions, chopped |

■ **In medium** bowl, stir together hoisin sauce, fish sauce, lime juice, sherry, ginger, sesame oil, sugar, lime zest, sambal oelek and garlic until well combined. Stir in mushrooms and eggplant. Let stand for 20 minutes or covered in refrigerator overnight.

■ **Place** noodles in deep bowl. Pour boiling water over noodles and let stand for 5 minutes; drain well and reserve.

■ **In small** bowl or measuring cup, stir together stock and cornstarch.

■ **Drain** eggplant and mushrooms, reserving marinade. Heat vegetable oil in wok or deep skillet set over high heat until smoking. Add eggplant and mushrooms and cook, without stirring, for 2 minutes or until browned on one side. Stir in green pepper and cook, without stirring, for 2 minutes. Stir, then let cook, without stirring, for 2 minutes. Stir once more and cook, without stirring, another 2 minutes. (If you stir too often, the vegetables won't become a deep golden brown.)

■ **Make** a well by pushing vegetables up sides of pan; stir stock and pour into well. Add marinade and cook, stirring, for 1 minute or until thickened. Toss to coat vegetables well. Add noodles and cook, tossing, for 2 minutes or until noodles are heated through.

■ **Transfer** to heated platter or shallow serving dish and sprinkle with cashews and green onions.

*Makes 4 servings.*

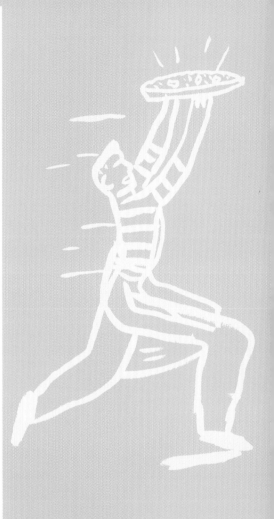

# CHILI WITH PASTA AND TWO BEANS

Here's a power meal for when you're skiing, skating or just want something that will stick to your ribs. The combination of beans, pasta and veggies makes this a healthful vegetarian lunch or dinner.

| | |
|---|---|
| 1 tbsp | vegetable oil |
| 2 | onions, chopped |
| 2 | cloves garlic, minced |
| 1 | each red and green pepper, diced |
| 1 tbsp | chili powder |
| 2 tsp | ground cumin |
| 1 tsp | ground coriander |
| 3/4 tsp | salt |
| 1/2 tsp | pepper |
| 1/2 tsp | dried oregano |
| 1 | can (28 oz/796 mL) tomatoes, chopped |
| 1 cup | each cooked black beans and kidney beans |
| 1/4 cup | chopped pickled cascabel peppers |
| 1 1/2 cups | cooked farfalle (3.5 oz dry) |
| 1/2 cup | fresh or thawed frozen corn kernels |
| 1/4 cup | chopped fresh coriander or parsley |
| | Sour cream |
| | Shredded aged Cheddar cheese |

■ **Heat** oil in large deep skillet or wok set over medium heat; add onions and cook, stirring occasionally, for 5 minutes or until softened. Stir in garlic, red and green peppers, chili powder, cumin, ground coriander, salt, pepper and oregano; cook, stirring often, for 10 minutes.

■ **Stir** in tomatoes, black beans, kidney beans and pickled peppers. Bring to a boil; reduce heat and simmer for 15 minutes or until thickened. Stir in pasta and corn and cook for 3 minutes or until heated through. Remove from heat and stir in fresh coriander. Taste and adjust seasoning if necessary. Serve topped with a dollop of sour cream and a sprinkling of Cheddar cheese.

*Makes 4 to 6 servings.*

**Cascabel peppers** are long, pale green horn-shaped peppers that have a medium hot taste and a crisp, thin flesh. They are available in most large chain grocery stores.

# One-Pan Gingered Ratatouille and Ditali

Ditali are a cute little tube-shaped pasta that blend in nicely with the diced vegetables called for in this dish. If you can't find it, choose tubetti, little shells or, in a pinch, elbow macaroni.

| | |
|---|---|
| 6 oz | ditali or other short pasta |
| 2 tbsp | olive oil |
| 1/2 cup | finely chopped red onion |
| 2 | cloves garlic, minced |
| 1/2 cup | cubed peeled eggplant |
| 1/2 cup | finely chopped zucchini |
| 1/2 cup | red pepper |
| 1/3 cup | fresh or thawed frozen corn kernels |
| 2 tbsp | aged balsamic vinegar |
| 1 tbsp | tamari |
| 1/2 tsp | each salt and pepper |
| 1 tbsp | grated gingerroot |
| 1 | can (19 oz/540 mL) tomatoes |
| 1/2 cup | cooked black beans |
| 1/4 cup | chopped fresh basil |
| 1/4 cup | grated Asiago or Parmesan cheese |

heat oil

■ **In large** pot of boiling salted water, cook pasta 8 to 10 minutes or until al dente. Drain well and reserve.

■ **Meanwhile**, heat 1 tbsp of the oil in nonstick skillet or wok set over medium heat; add onion and cook, stirring often, for 5 minutes or until softened. Add garlic and cook for 1 minute. Add remaining oil and increase heat to high; add eggplant, zucchini, red pepper and corn. Cook, stirring often, for 3 to 4 minutes or until vegetables are well browned. Stir in balsamic vinegar and tamari; cook, tossing, until vegetables are glazed and excess moisture has cooked off. Season with salt and pepper.

■ **Push** ingredients up sides of pan to make a well. Stir in ginger and tomatoes, breaking up with back of spoon; bring to a boil and cook, stirring tomatoes occasionally, for 5 minutes or until thickened. Add pasta and stir until vegetables, tomatoes and pasta are well combined.

■ **Remove** from heat and stir in beans, basil and cheese. Taste and adjust seasoning if necessary.

*Makes 4 to 6 servings.*

**Balsamic vinegar** is made in Modena, Italy. Cookery writer and teacher Marcella Hazan first introduced this mellow, sweet flavored vinegar to North America. Because balsamic vinegar adds not only tang but depth and sweetness to almost anything to which it is added, it has become widely popular.

To make balsamic vinegar, grape juice is concentrated over a low flame and then aged for 5 to 20 years in a series of wooden barrels.

# Pasta Shells with Bombay Sauce

Even people who aren't typically fond of Indian food enjoy this hearty and aromatic dish.

| | |
|---|---|
| 2 tbsp | vegetable oil |
| 1 | onion, chopped |
| 1 tbsp | mild Indian curry paste |
| 1/2 tsp | each ground ginger, cumin and chili powder |
| 1/2 tsp | salt |
| 2 cups | cubed peeled butternut squash |
| 2 | large carrots, cut into large chunks |
| 2 | cloves garlic, minced |
| 1 cup | vegetable stock |
| 1/2 | zucchini, chopped |
| 1 cup | cooked chickpeas |
| 1/4 cup | sultana raisins |
| 1 tsp | lemon juice |
| 6 oz | small pasta shells |
| 2 tbsp | toasted whole blanched almonds (see page 76) |
| | Plain yogurt |

■ **Heat** oil in large saucepan set over medium heat; add onion and cook, stirring occasionally, for 5 minutes or until softened. Add curry paste, ginger, cumin, chili powder and salt. Cook, stirring, for 2 minutes or until very fragrant.

■ **Add** squash, carrots, garlic and stock. Bring to a boil; reduce heat and simmer, partly covered, for 5 minutes or until vegetables are just beginning to become tender. Stir in zucchini, chickpeas and raisins; cook, partly covered, for 2 minutes or until vegetables are tender and stock is reduced to about $1/4$ cup. Remove from heat and stir in lemon juice.

■ **Meanwhile**, in large pot of boiling salted water, cook pasta for 8 to 10 minutes or until al dente. Drain well and stir into vegetable mixture; taste and adjust seasoning if necessary. Sprinkle with almonds. Serve with yogurt on the side.

*Makes 4 to 6 servings.*

**Variation**
**Spicy Bombay Vegetable Sauce:** Add 2 finely diced red chilies along with the garlic, or substitute hot Indian curry paste for mild and serve with chutney as well as yogurt.

# ACKNOWLEDGMENTS

A project like this one requires the input and expertise of so many people that it seems unfair to have only one name on the front cover. For instance, without the creativity and initiative of Denise Schon, this book would never have been written in the first place. Likewise, Doug Pepper's belief in the viability of the project was essential for *Noodles Express* to be published.

For her eye for detail, meticulous recipe-testing skills and excellent palate, I owe Beatrice Damore a shopping basket full of thanks, too. Ready tasters and moral supporters Martin and Oliver Kouprie, Jeanne McCauley, Lydia Caruso and the Ballotta family provided the feedback and encouragement needed to make these recipes appealing to a broad range of people. Non-noodle fans Vince and Doug McCauley helped to prevent these recipes from getting, and I quote, "too weird."

And, of course, a book doesn't get published without the hard work of many people who toil behind the scenes. My thanks and admiration go out to designer Linda Gustafson, illustrators Huntley/Muir, Hal Roth, copy editor Shaun Oakey and to Anna Barron and Eva Quan.

Lastly, thank you to anyone reading these pages, for without you, there truly would be no *Noodles Express*.

# INDEX

Almonds: Asian pesto, 74–75; bucatini with tamari-almond sauce, 62; goat cheese pasta salad, 35

Apples, green curry salad, 30

Arugula, and potatoes with orecchiette, 70

Asian pears, about, 87

Asian-style: noodle soup, 26–27; pasta primavera, 67; pear salad with cranberry dressing, 86–87; pesto, 74–75

Asparagus: fettuccine, 102–3; saffron sauce, 81; and sweet pepper salad, 38

Avocado: about, 34; pasta salad, 34

Balsamic vinegar, about, 153

Beans. See Black beans; Green beans; Kidney beans; Yellow beans

Bean starch noodles, about, 12

Beet leaves: linguine with, 118–19; and potatoes with orecchiette, 70

Beets: how to cook, 41; with linguine, 118–19; with noodles, 112–13; and orecchiette salad, 40–41; ruby-stained fusilli, 92–93

Black beans: chili with pasta and, 150–51; pasta salad, 34 See also Fermented black beans

Bok choy, hot mustard sauce chow mein, 56

Bombay sauce: pasta with, 154–55; vegetable, 155

Broad noodles with mushroom port sauce, 136–37

Broccoli: macaroni and cheese, 65; with skoo-bi-do, 104–5; soba salad, 36; spaghetti and vegetable toss, 96–97; and tofu stir-fry, 110–11

Bucatini: about, 12; goat cheese-almond salad, 35; salad with greens, 35; with tamari-almond sauce, 62

Buttermilk: about, 79; -walnut quick gratin, 78–79

Capellini: Pangaea, 128–29; with spinach in chili-ginger sauce, 72–73

Capers, about, 71

Caramelized onion, green bean and fusilli toss, 146–47

Cardamom, about, 139

Carrot juice, gnocchi with cardamom sauce, 138–39

Carrots, pasta with Bombay sauce, 154–55

Cascabel peppers, about, 151

Cheese, macaroni and, 64–65

Cherry tomatoes, noodles Marengo, 140–41

Chickpeas, pasta with Bombay sauce, 154–55

Chili with pasta and beans, 150–51

Chili powder, about, 123

Chow mein: about, 12, 59; Dan Dan noodles, 63; hot, 116–17; in hot mustard sauce, 56; salad with citrus dressing, 32–33; sesame, 54–55; stir-fry, 57; Szechwan tofu supper, 100–1; Thai red curry–coconut stir-fry, 58–59; in Thai red curry paste broth, 31; vegetable, 60–61

Clamato juice, ramen soup, 23

Coconut milk: about, 89; jade stir-fry, 98–99; Malaysian salad, 134–35; noodle soup, 88–89; rice noodles with vegetables, 106–7; spinach noodles with Thai green curry paste, 82; Thai red curry–coconut stir-fry, 58–59

Coriander, about, 75

Corn: Mexican-style pasta dinner, 122–23; spaghetti and vegetable toss, 96–97

Cous cous: about, 109; with pomegranate molasses in pita, 46–47

Cranberries, Asian pear salad, 86–87

Cream: fettuccine, 71, 80–81; Mexican-style pasta dinner, 122–23; noodles with fennel in sauce, 112–13; pasta with spring onion sauce, 126–27; spaghetti with minted pea sauce, 83; tagliatelle with wasabi cream sauce, 51

Creamy Mexican pasta dinner, 122–23

Creamy wasabi pasta and bean salad, 45

Cucumber, fettuccine, 71

Curry(ied): about Indian curry paste, 43; about Thai green curry paste, 30; about Thai red curry paste, 31; broth with noodles, 31; orzo salad, 42–43; pasta and apple salad, 30; pasta with

Bombay sauce, 154–55; spinach noodles, 82

Daikon:
about, 33; chow mein salad, 32–33
Dana's Dan Dan noodles, 63
Ditali:
about, 12; ratatouille and, 152–53
Dressing:
champagne–saffron, 38; with sun–dried tomatoes, 35

Easy Asian-style pasta primavera, 67
Easy cous cous salad, 108–9
Easy and fresh fettuccine, 71
Egg noodles Marengo, 140–41
Eggplant:
marinated with mushrooms and noodles, 148–49; Middle Eastern sauce, 144–45; ratatouille, 152–53
Eggs:
chow mein, 61; noodle quiche, 142–43; orzo goreng, 48–49; pad Thai, 131
Elegant mushroom stroganoff, 136

Farfalle:
Asian pear salad, 86–87; sweet and sour peppers stir-fry, 120–21
Fast and fresh fettuccine, 71
Fennel, with noodles, 112–13
Fermented black beans, 68, 69

Fettuccine, 71; asparagus, 102–3; sultana, 80–81
Fiery coconut noodle soup, 88–89
Firecracker noodles, 116–17
Fish sauce, about, 143
Five-minute tomato ramen soup, 23
Flame-thrower noodles, 117
French onion, macaroni and cheese, 65
Fresh pea and egg noodle soup, 22
Fusilli:
with beets, 92–93; caramelized onion and green bean toss, 146–47; and kidney bean salad, 45

Gnocchi with carrot cardamom sauce, 138–39
Goat cheese-almond pasta salad, 35
Greek-style tortellini salad, 39
Green beans:
onion and fusilli toss, 146–47; and spinach noodles, 82; Thai red curry paste broth, 31
Green curry:
and green apple salad, 30 See also Thai green curry paste
Green onions, radiatore with, 126–27
Green peas. See Snap peas; Snow peas

Herbs, pesto, 74–75

Honey-glazed snap peas and noodles, 66
Hot mustard sauce chow mein, 56
Hot and sour soup and noodle supper, 20–21

Indian curry paste, about, 43

Ketjap manis, about, 49
Kidney beans:
chili with pasta and, 150–51; and pasta salad, 45

Leek, soba and shiitake soup, 90–91
Lemongrass, about, 25
Lentils:
about, 44; and macaroni salad, 44
Linguine:
Asian pesto, 74–75; with beet greens, 118–19; in mushroom ginger broth, 28–29; salad with greens, 35

Macaroni:
and cheese, 64–65; and lentil salad, 44
Malaysian coconut salad, 134–35
Mango:
about, 50; and rice noodle salad, 50
Maui onions, about, 147
Mexican-style pasta dinner, 122–23
Middle Eastern–style penne with eggplant sauce, 144–45

Miki noodles, honey-glazed snap peas and, 66
Minced prawns in spice:
about, 131; pad Thai, 130–31
Mushrooms:
broad noodles with port sauce, 136–37; hot and sour noodle soup, 20–21; noodle quiche, 142–43; and noodles in ginger broth, 28–29; noodles Marengo, 140–41; and noodle snack in lemon broth, 25; stir-fry with snow peas, 68–69; stroganoff, 136

Napa cabbage:
coconut jade stir-fry, 98–99; Dan Dan noodles, 63; sweet pea and noodle soup, 22; tofu and rice noodles, 94–95
Nasi goreng, about, 48
Noodle nests, sweet pea soup, 22
Noodles:
with fennel and creamy star anise–beet sauce, 112–13; in mushroom ginger broth, 28–29
Nuts, to toast, 76

One-pan gingered ratatouille and ditali, 152–53
Onions:
about, 127, 147; macaroni and cheese, 65; to peel, 141; radiatore with green onion sauce, 126–27

Oranges:
 -infused beet and orecchiette salad, 40–41; Shanghai noodles in orange sauce, 124–25
Orecchiette:
 about, 70; and beet salad, 40–41; with peas and potatoes, 70
Orzo:
 goreng, 48–49; salad curry, 42–43; spice tent, 76
Oyster sauce, about, 115

Pacific Rim stove-top noodle quiche, 142–43
Pad Thai, 130–31
Painted desert pasta salad, 34
Pan-Asian penne all'arrabbiata, 114–15
Pangaea capellini, 128–29
Parmesan cheese:
 tagliatelle with wasabi cream sauce, 51; See also Parmigiano-Reggiano
Parmigiano-Reggiano:
 about, 77; buttermilk-walnut quick gratin, 78–79; squash ravioli meunière, 77
Pasta:
 with Bombay sauce, 154–55; primavera, Asian-style, 67
Pasta with Spring Onion Sauce, 126
Pears, Asian salad, 86–87
Peas. See Snap peas; Sweet peas
Penne:
 all'arrabbiata, 114–15; asparagus and sweet pepper salad, 38;

with Middle Eastern eggplant sauce, 144–45; Thai green curry paste and apple salad, 30
Pepper, about, 73
Peppers. See Sweet peppers
Pesto, Asian-style, 74–75
Pickled ginger, about, 51
Pita breads, stuffed with cous cous, 46–47
Plaid noodles, 118–19
Pomegranate cous cous in pitas, 46–47
Pomegranate molasses, about, 47
Protein-boost Mexican pasta dinner, 123
Puréeing, about, 93

Quick skillet macaroni and cheese, 64–65

Radiatore:
 about, 12; with spring onion sauce, 126–27
Radicchio, pasta salad, 35
Ramen:
 about, 12, 23; Asian-style soup, 26–27; and mushroom snack, 25; soup, 24; tomato soup, 23
Rapini:
 about, 105; with skoo-bi-do, 104–5
Ratatouille and ditali, 152–53
Ravioli, meunière, 77
Red curry. See Thai red curry paste
Red peppers. See Sweet peppers

Rice noodles:
 about, 12; with Asian roasted red pepper sauce, 52–53; coconut jade stir-fry, 98–99; hot and sour soup, 20–21; Malaysian coconut salad, 134–35; pad Thai, 130–31; with Thai eggplant and mushrooms, 148–49; with tofu and vegetables, 94–95
Rice vermicelli, and mango salad, 50
Ruby-stained fusilli, 92–93

Saffron:
 about, 81; fettuccine sultana, 80–81
Salad:
 Asian pear, 86–87; beet, 40–41; black bean and avocado, 34; chow mein, 32–33; cous cous, 108–9; fusilli and kidney bean, 45; goat cheese–almond pasta, 35; macaroni and lentil, 44; Malaysian coconut, 134–35; mango and rice noodle, 50; pasta with greens, 35; soba with broccoli, 36; sweet potato and pasta, 37; Thai green curry paste and apple, 30; tortellini Greek-style, 39
Sambal oelek, about, 125
Sesame noodles, 54–55
Shanghai noodles in orange sauce, 124–25

Shiitake:
 leek and soba soup, 90–91; and noodles in ginger broth, 28–29
Shrimp paste, about, 99
Skoo-bi-do:
 about, 12, 104; Mexican pasta dinner, 122–23; with rapini, 104–5
Snacks, mushroom and noodle, 25
Snap peas:
 and noodles, 66
 See also Snow peas
Snow peas:
 Asian noodle soup, 26–27; chow mein salad, 32–33; chow mein stir-fry, 57; Malaysian coconut salad, 134–35; and mushroom stir-fry in black bean sauce, 68–69; Pangaea capellini, 128–29
 See also Snap peas
Soba:
 about, 12–13, 36; coconut soup, 88–89; leek and shiitake soup, 90–91; salad with broccoli, 36
Soup:
 Asian, 26–27; hot and sour noodle, 20–21; leek, soba and shiitake, 90–91; noodle and mushroom, 28–29; ramen, 24; sweet pea and noodle, 22; Thai red curry paste broth, 31; tomato ramen, 23
Soy sauce, about, 27

Spaghetti:
    with minted pea sauce, 83; and vegetable toss, 96–97
Spanish onions, about, 147
Spice tent orzo, 76
Spicy Bombay vegetable sauce, 155
Spicy spaghetti and vegetable toss, 96–97
Spinach:
    with capellini in chili-ginger sauce, 72–73; and potatoes with orecchiette, 70; tomato ramen soup, 23
Spinach Noodles with Spicy Green Curry, 82
Squash:
    pasta with Bombay sauce, 154–55; ravioli meunière, 77
Star anise, about, 91
stir-fry:
    broccoli and tofu with rice ribbons, 110–11; chow mein, 57; coconut jade, 98–99; honey-glazed snap peas and noodles, 66; snow pea and mushroom, 68–69; sweet and sour peppers and farfalle, 120–21; Thai red curry–coconut, 58–59
Stock, about, 14–15
Sun-dried tomatoes:
    about, 62; dressing, 35
Sweet peas:
    and noodle soup, 22; and potatoes with orecchiette, 70; spaghetti with, 83; tomato ramen soup, 23

Sweet peppers:
    asparagus salad, 38; chow mein stir-fry, 57; farfalle stir-fry, 120–21; pasta salad, 35; to roast, 53; roasted, with noodles, 52–53; spaghetti and vegetable toss, 96–97
Sweet potato and pasta salad, 37
Sweet and sour peppers, and farfalle stir-fry, 120–21
Swiss chard:
    noodles, 118–19; and potatoes with orecchiette, 70
Szechwan:
    pepper, about, 73; tofu and noodle supper, 100–1
Tabasco sauce, about, 14
Tagliatelle with wasabi cream sauce, 51
Tahini, about, 55
Tamari, about, 21
Thai green curry paste:
    about, 30; green apple salad, 30; spinach noodles with, 82
Thai marinated eggplant and mushrooms with noodles, 148–49
Thai red curry paste:
    about, 58, 31; broth with noodles, 31; –coconut stir-fry, 58–59
Tofu:
    about, 111; and broccoli stir-fry, 110–11; hot and sour noodle soup, 20–21; pad Thai, 130–31; red curry broth with noodles, 31; rice

noodles and vegetables, 94–95; Szechwan noodle supper, 100–1
Tomato(es):
    macaroni and lentil salad, 44; noodle quiche, 142–43; saffron sauce, 81; soba salad with broccoli, 36; See also Sun-dried tomatoes
Toronto meets Singapore Noodles, 94
Tortellini, Greek-style salad, 39
Truffle oil, about, 136
Truffles, about, 136
20-minute vegetarian pad Thai, 130–31

Udon:
    about, 13; with fennel and creamy star anise–beet sauce, 112–13

V8 juice, ramen soup, 23
Vegetables:
    Asian-style pasta primavera, 67; chow mein, 60–61; cous cous salad, 108–9; ravioli meunière, 77; with rice noodles, 106–7; zippy ramen, 24
Vidalia onions:
    about, 147; green bean and fusilli toss, 146–47
Vietnamese rice sticks, with vegetables and peanut sauce, 106–7

Vinaigrette, champagne-saffron, 38
Walnuts, buttermilk-walnut quick gratin, 78–79
Wasabi, about, 45
Water chestnuts, peppers and chow mein stir-fry, 57
Watercress, sweet potato and pasta salad, 37
Wild mushrooms, broad noodles with port sauce, 136–37
Wood ear mushrooms, about, 29

Yellow beans, red curry broth, 31
Yellow peppers. See Sweet peppers

Zesty pasta salad, with greens, 35
Zippy ramen, 24
Zucchini:
    noodle quiche, 142–43; pasta with Bombay sauce, 154–55; ratatouille, 152–53; red curry–coconut stir-fry, 58–59